FIND YOUR
brave

IT WAS ALWAYS IN YOU
IT'S NOW TIME TO FIND IT

MICHELLE JONES

Copyright © 2025 by Michelle Jones

All rights reserved. No part of this publication may be reproduced, distributed, or transmitted in any form or by any means, including photocopying, recording, or other electronic or mechanical methods, without the prior written permission of the publisher, except in the case of brief quotations embodied in critical reviews and certain other noncommercial uses permitted by copyright law.

Scripture quotations marked (NKJV) are taken from the New King James Version®. Copyright © 1982 by Thomas Nelson. Used by permission. All rights reserved.

Ordering Information:

Available where all books are sold or online at online book retailers.

Printed in the United States of America

ISBN 978-1-7341741-4-4
      978-1-7341741-5-1

First Edition
14 13 12 11 10 / 10 9 8 7 6 5 4 3 2 1

TABLE OF CONTENTS

ACKNOWLEDGMENTS...i

CHAPTER 1 .... **1**
YOU ARE GOING TO MAKE IT

CHAPTER 2 .... **13**
WHAT ARE YOU SPEAKING?

CHAPTER 3 .... **25**
THE BATTLE IS GOD'S, NOT YOURS

CHAPTER 4 .... **35**
FEAR IS A LIAR

CHAPTER 5... **47**
STOP PLAYING MIND GAMES

CHAPTER 6 .... **59**
BEAUTY FROM ASHES

CHAPTER 7... **71**
JOY IN THE MIDDLE OF PAIN

CHAPTER 8 .... **83**
PRAISE GOD ON CREDIT

CHAPTER 9 .... **93**
DELAY IS NOT DENIAL

CHAPTER 10..**107**
YOU ARE STRONGER THAN YOU THINK

VERSES AND REFERENCES... **123**

ACKNOWLEDGMENTS

To my husband: Jamie, you are my whole world. You have always been my rock and my strength. Thank you for always believing in me and pushing me to be better. I love you.

To my three kids: Kristen, James, and Joshua: I am so proud of you. God has surely blessed me in an incredible way. I'm thankful to be your momma. You are all world-changers! Keep dreaming, keep believing, and keep Jesus first always. To my daughters-and son-in-love, Alexis, Armando, and soon-to-be Kristi: you are special and treasured.

To my grandbabies: Ember, Judah, Sunnie, Scarlett, Benaiah, Maverick, Elisha, Maddox, Shiloh, Honey, Myles, Maisie, and all the ones to come: I love you with every fiber of my being. I wrote this book for you - to help you understand how special you are to the Lord. You are brave, smart, and He has a special plan for your life. Please always remember,

Gigi and Pops love you. Keep Jesus first in your life!

To my momma and daddy: thank you for instilling in me a love for others, a strong work ethic, and the importance of staying humble. I'll see you again. I love you. To Misti, Philip, Makayla, Chance, and Colton: thank you for always believing in me. Phil and Wanda – thank you for loving me.

To Trinity Church: thank you for your love, support, and faithfulness. I love you and am so thankful to have you in my life.

Jesus, thank You for saving me, healing me, and rescuing me out of my mess. Thank you for my life, for my family, and for giving me the words to write this book. Thank you for the honor of preaching Your Word. I'm nothing without You.

CHAPTER 1

YOU ARE GOING TO MAKE IT

Have you ever heard someone say, "God will not give you more than you can handle?" I know I have, many times. While people mean well, that phrase simply isn't true. Valley seasons often bring more than we can handle on our own, and that's exactly why we need the Lord.

God never promised that life would be easy, but He promised to be with us. In 1 Corinthians 10:13, we are reminded: "*No temptation has overtaken you except such as is common to man; but God is faithful, who will not allow you to be tempted beyond what you are able, but with the temptation will also make the way of escape, that you may be able to bear it*" (NKJV). To be honest, there have been many times I've said,

"God, I cannot handle this. It's just too much."

Pain can feel overwhelming, and if you're walking through something painful right now, you know exactly what I mean. But I've learned that we can't live by what we feel. We have to live by what the Word of God says. Our feelings are fleeting and

> Trust
> in the
> Lord...

often misleading; they can influence us to depend on what is temporary and unstable.

God's Word, on the other hand, is steady and true. Scripture says, *"Trust in the Lord with all your heart, and lean not on your own understanding"* (Proverbs 3:5, NKJV). Feelings shift from day to day, sometimes even moment to moment, and are not a solid foundation for truth nor a reliable guide for how we should respond when we are hurt. And when we're hurting, we need something solid to stand on.

Life brings real pain. It hurts when someone walks away, when someone you love passes, when your job disappears, or when the past tries to haunt you. Emotions matter and how you process them matters. It is okay to feel sadness, anger, disappointment, even bitterness, but you cannot stay there. You were not meant to live in regret or shame. If you get stuck in the "why me?" mindset, you will miss the goodness of God that is right in front of you.

Jesus knows exactly how you feel and what you are experiencing. He lived a fully human life, and He experienced the range of emotions we now face. Jesus experienced sadness when He wept at Lazarus's tomb (John 11:35). He demonstrated righteous anger when He turned over tables in the temple (Matthew 21:12). He knows what heartbreak, betrayal, grief and frustration feels like. So yes—He understands what you may be feeling. That's why it's so important to be honest, not just with others, but with yourself and with God.

We often hide our struggles behind a smile. We become experts at playing the "*I am fine*" game; we say "I'm fine," when really, we're not. We walk into church, put on our Sunday best, and act like nothing's wrong. We pretend all is well, but pretending doesn't bring healing. Suppressing pain only makes it grow deeper. The enemy thrives in that hidden space, feeding you lies, and keeping you stuck, but God sees through the mask and knows your heart. He longs to bring healing and freedom to the places you've tried to hide.

Whatever you're facing in your life, know this: God sees you. He intimately knows your pain. He loves you, He's for you, and He has a plan for your life that is filled with hope and a future. He wants to prosper you and bless you. God says, *"For I know the thoughts that I think toward you," says the Lord, "thoughts of peace and not of evil, to give you a future and a hope"* (Jeremiah 29:11, NKJV). So let me remind you—you will make it. This chapter of your life is not the complete story. It's just one page.

Your current defeat will not overtake you and is not how your story ends. God's promises are still "Yes" and "Amen" (2 Corinthians 1:20, NKJV). I know it feels like you can't survive this, believe me, I know this feeling all too well. But I also know God will carry you through. Holding on to that promise would become more real to me than I ever expected.

> Your current defeat... is not how your story ends.

It was a Friday afternoon when my daughter Kristen and I went out for a nice lunch. We had just sat down at the restaurant when my phone rang. It was my doctor.

"Mrs. Jones, are you sitting down?" he asked. My heart dropped. That's never something you want to hear from your doctor.

Just two weeks earlier, I went in for a "routine" mammogram. Nothing seemed off and I walked in as I have in the past, not expecting anything out of the ordinary. The room was always dark and a little scary, but I had no reason to fear, except this time the exam took longer and they asked for an ultrasound right after. Despite the unusual duration and the ultrasound that followed, I maintained that this was nothing more than just a routine exam. As I lay on the table, the specialist came in and said,

"You need a biopsy."

"A biopsy?" I replied, "Why would I need *that*?"

They explained they observed something suspicious, and it required further investigation. I had heard of biopsies before, but I never really knew how they worked. I scheduled the biopsy and tried to remain calm and positive. They scheduled the appointment for just a few days later. I remember walking into that appointment thinking,

"This is just a precaution, they won't find anything, and I'll go home."

Jamie, my husband, and I prayed and declared God's Word before the appointment, and we believed God was going to work it out. The biopsy itself was quick, they said they would call me with the results. I went home to wait. Waiting was the hardest part. So, when the doctor called just two days later, as I was now sitting in the restaurant with my daughter, I felt the weight of the unknown pressing in.

"I have the results back from the biopsy." He said just before he uttered the three words, I never thought I would hear.

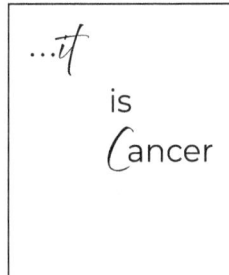

"IT IS CANCER."

Those three words changed everything. I felt the air leave my lungs. I could not speak. So many thoughts raced through my mind.

"How could this be possible?

"I don't have a family history of breast cancer."

"I am healthy, aren't I too young?"

The whole ordeal felt like a nightmare I could not escape. Across the table, Kristen looked at me with concern, but I was speechless. *What was I going to do now?* So many thoughts yet so little words. What would I say to my daughter?

"We have to go" is all I could say as we quietly excused ourselves from the restaurant. My heart raced as we got into the car. I reminded myself to remain strong, if only for Kristen. I vividly remember the concerned look on her face. There was no denying *something* was wrong, but I don't think anything could have prepared her for what I would say next.

I shared with her the three dreaded words the doctor spoke to me and added *"But our God will be with us. It is going to be okay."* Honestly, I really did not know for sure if I believed that I would be *okay*, the only thing I did know for sure is that God was not going to leave me now.

> ...One of the *hardest* things I've *Ever* done

Jamie, who was on a fishing trip with our boys, happened to call a few minutes later. I told him I needed him to come home as soon as possible. I did not want to give him the news over the phone although he already knew I was expecting a call from the doctor. Somehow, I think he already knew it wasn't good news, my voice gave it away. After we talked, we brought all the kids together in our bedroom to tell them what the doctor had said.

Breaking the news to our kids was one of the hardest things I've ever done. The weight of that moment was overwhelming, and every part of me wanted to shield them from the pain. In fact, my first thought was to keep it from everyone. I didn't want to tell my family, my church, or even my friends. It crushed me to think I might bring pain to the people I love so much.

But this wasn't just my journey, it was ours. I knew our whole family would go through this together. As a momma, my instinct is to keep them safe, to shelter them from all the bad things of the world. But I realized I couldn't protect them from everything. I had to trust that God was going to do something big in all our lives. Who was I to take away from the testimony He was writing? I had to believe that even in this, God would be glorified.

That night in the shower, I cried and prayed. I felt completely broken, helpless, alone, and exhausted. Then in the stillness, I heard a voice:

"Are you going to trust Me?"

Startled, I opened my eyes and looked around. Was someone there? Had I really heard that? My mind raced to make sense of it. Then I heard it again, even clearer:

> *...in the stillness, I heard a voice: "Are you going to trust Me?"*

"Are you going to trust Me?"

This time, I knew it was God. I had never heard His audible voice like that before and I haven't since. But right there, in my deepest pain, He met *me*. Through trembling lips, I whispered back,

"Yes, Lord. I will trust You."

Trusting God is easy to say, but hard to live out. I did not understand the "why." I didn't believe God caused the cancer—of course not, but I knew He had allowed it. Oftentimes we spend our lives trying to figure out the "*why.*" But in this valley, I learned something important: chasing the "why" can rob you of seeing the good that God is working in the middle of your pain.

The days that followed were filled with endless tests and appointments. I felt like I was caught in a whirlwind. The world spun around me, and all I could do was try to survive. I would try to catch my breath, but it felt almost impossible.

What do you do when your whole world is suddenly turned upside down? One minute, you are out with your daughter enjoying a beautiful day—the next, you are faced with a deadly diagnosis. It feels like you are trapped in a bubble. The world keeps moving, but you're stuck behind invisible walls no one else seems to see. It is hard to breathe. Even when people talk to you, their words feel distant, like they're floating past you. All you can hear are those three words echoing in your mind: *"It is cancer."*

At my first oncology appointment, it all hit me. The hospital carried a tangible weight you could feel the moment you stepped into the waiting room. I scanned the room and saw sadness, hopelessness, and despair etched into faces around me. People who, just like me, were fighting battles I was only beginning to understand. I remember thinking, "I should not be here."

> God, I cannot do This...

I sat down in the waiting room, feeling numb. As I waited for my name to be called, the weight of it all pressed down on me. I wondered, "How did I get to this point?" I closed my eyes and whispered, "God, I cannot do this. It feels too hard." I felt Him gently whisper back, *"No, you can't...but I can."*
I held on to that promise as they called my name to go back and see the doctor.

The oncologist had a strong yet kind demeanor, yet his words were foreign. He used unfamiliar terms and although we were all in the same room, I was disconnected. As he scheduled more tests, I was overloaded with all the information coming at me. I returned to my original thoughts and continued to wonder, "How did I end up here?" It was all happening so fast.

After the doctor finished with his portion, he turned me over to the nurse who remained with me throughout the entire visit. He said:

> "I will let you go over all the details of the upcoming appointments with her."

The nurse was kind and so sweet toward me. She pulled up a chair and sat next to me as she reviewed my plan of care. When she was done explaining, something unexpected happened—she wrapped her arms around me and said,

"You are going to make it."

Caught off guard by her words and kind gesture, I looked at her with tears in my eyes, I was speechless as she continued:

> "I have been in this a long time, and I have seen patients come and go from this office. I can tell by your faith that you are going to make it. You have the right mindset."

She gently touched my long blond hair and said,

> "You will lose all your hair—but it will grow back. You will make it through this."

Despite my fear and anxiety, my husband and I never lost sight of God. I did not know how it would turn out, but I knew God would be with me. His Word says in Isaiah 53:5, *"By His stripes we are healed"* (NKJV). The Word does not say we *might* be healed, or that only good people will be healed. No, it says, "We *are* healed."

I believe that God used that sweet nurse to remind me of His promise and to keep trusting Him through every step of this journey. Now I am here to

> Being
> *Brave*
> isn't a
> *feeling*
> it's an
> *Action*

tell you, my friend, you *will* make it through this. I know it feels like too much, but God will see you through. You might feel weak, but God says, *"Have I not commanded you? Be strong and of good courage; do not be afraid, nor be dismayed, for the Lord your God is with you wherever you go"* (Joshua 1:9, NKJV).

Being brave isn't a feeling, it's an action. It's taking one step forward when everything in you wants to turn back. It's drawing strength from God when you have nothing left. God is with you in the valley. That is where He prepares and promotes. The mountaintop reveals the promise, but the valley is where God lays the foundation.

I have never forgotten that nurse's words or God's voice in the shower. When darkness tries to creep in, I hold onto what He said. I do not speak what I see, but I speak what He said. In a world full of noise, I choose to declare God's truth. God says I am healed, and to fear not. The enemy wants to kick you when you're down, but he only wins if you let him. So many times, we spend our energy trying to fix the problem on our own or we try to help God fix it, but God doesn't need our help; He needs our trust and obedience. The question is, will *you* trust Him?

Scripture says, *"Trust in the Lord with all your heart, and lean not on your own understanding; in all your ways acknowledge Him, and He shall direct your paths"* (Proverbs 3:5, NKJV). Stop trying to figure it all out. I remember the night after that shower. I knelt by my bed, feeling broken and scared as I exhaustedly prayed, asking God,

"Why me?"

and in that moment of questioning, I heard him say,

"*Why not you?*"

That deeply hit me. God wanted to use me for His glory. Why not me? He wants to use somebody, why not me? And, He wants to use you too.

The more I leaned into God, the more I realized there was much to know about God. I believe one of the enemy's biggest lies is, "You will not make it through this." He tries to cause fear. If you do not speak to that fear and take it captive, those fearful thoughts will only grow louder and stronger. Replace the enemy's lies with God's truth. The truth is, you are mighty through Jesus. You will make it!

In the coming chapters, I will share some of the hardest moments I've had to endure. My response to adversity had a significant impact on my life. My prayer is that through sharing these moments with you, they will help you gain perspective and strengthen your response in the face of trials and tribulations.

My advice is don't speak what you see, speak what He said. God's promises are still true and His plans for your life will come to pass.

So, what are you speaking over your life today?

CHAPTER 2

WHAT ARE YOU SPEAKING?

I was around 15 years old; I can still remember it like it was yesterday—standing in my bathroom, getting ready for school one morning. Out of the corner of my eye, I saw something shift in the mirror's reflection. When I turned around, there was something black lurking in the corner of my bathroom. As I inched closer, I quickly realized it was a snake! So, I did what any normal 15-year-old girl would do in that situation: I screamed my head off and jumped onto the bathroom counter. My daddy, who was in the other room, came running the moment he heard my panicked screams; however, the lock kept him from getting to me.

"Open the door! Are you alright?" he shouted.
"No, I am NOT all right!" I screamed back.
"There is a giant snake in the bathroom!"
"A giant what?" he asked. "How big is it? What color?"
I told him it was huge—maybe around five feet long—black and scary. With the door locked and

panic rising, I heard my daddy's voice on the other side, trying to talk me down, and urging me to unlock the door, but to do that, I'd have to walk right past the giant snake.

Eventually, my daddy broke down the door and found me sitting on the bathroom countertop, still crying my eyes out. I pointed to the snake, expecting him to be equally horrified. Instead, my daddy picked up the snake and said,

"Is this what all the ruckus was about?"
Then, with a small grin, he added,

"This is a baby black snake. It is not five feet long—it's maybe 12 inches long."

> When we let fear take over... it begins to feel Larger than Life.

What? I thought. It's just *a baby snake*? It did not matter to me, it was terrifying. It didn't belong in my bathroom, and it scared me out of my mind. Even now, I remember that moment. I laugh about it, but back then I was convinced it was going to kill me and that is the deceptive power of fear. When we let fear take over, the thing causing it begins to feel larger than life. It grows in our minds until it feels overwhelming, even if it's much smaller in reality.

Sometimes we face seasons in life that feel so much bigger than anything we can conquer. It can seem like we will never make it through. Whether it's a strained marriage, a child who's lost their way, or a health crisis that leaves you shaken, these moments can feel larger than life. And the more we let our thoughts wander, the more likely we are to start believing the lies the enemy wants us to accept.

What we dwell on has a huge impact on our lives. If our minds are consumed by negative thoughts, they will destroy our faith. If we think our marriage won't survive, our children will never return to the Lord, or this sickness will end in death, we are setting ourselves up for failure.

Proverbs 18:21 reminds us, *"Death and life are in the power of the tongue."* What you speak and what you allow yourself to think—has power. So, ask yourself: What are you speaking?

You have the power to speak death or life over your situation. Which one are you speaking? You must take charge of your thoughts, or your thoughts will take charge of you. When you are facing mountains in front of you, are you going to choose life, or are you going to choose death? You have the power, through Jesus, to choose. You may not have control over what happens to you, but you do have control over how you respond.

Take the story of Joshua and the wall of Jericho. Joshua led the Israelites into the Promised Land. They crossed the Jordan River into Canaan, but soon realized they were not alone. Jericho stood before them. This city was massive. If we are not careful, what we see can overshadow what God has said.

The Bible says the gates of Jericho were tightly shut; no one was allowed to go in or out. God told Joshua to take the city, but he had to follow His instructions exactly. He told Joshua to march silently around the city once a day for six days, and on the seventh day to march around it seven times. Then, at the sound of a long trumpet blast, the people were to give a great shout.

As Joshua stood before the heavily fortified city, he had to choose between trusting God's plan or giving in to fear. The walls of Jericho were imposing. They were made of thick, heavy mud bricks, thirty feet high and twenty feet thick. Some houses were even built on top of them. To the Israelites, it looked impossible. I am sure their minds wandered to the worst-case scenario. What they saw in the natural looked terrifying. How could they possibly conquer such a place? But sometimes, the answer God provides is nothing like we expect.

> "What I have for you is so big..."

Isaiah 55:8-9 reminds us, *"For My thoughts are not your thoughts, Nor are your ways My ways,"* says the Lord. *"For as the heavens are higher than the earth, So are My ways higher than your ways, and My thoughts than your thoughts"* (NKJV). God is saying, *"What I have for you is so big you cannot even imagine it."* Don't let what you see, stop you from what He said; God's strategies often defy human logic, because He sees what we cannot.

Maybe your walls feel impossible, too. You might wonder, *"How can I overcome this?"* It feels too big and too hard. You think about all the ways you have messed up in your life. But when God steps into your situation, walls fall down. I have heard it said,

"Whatever you are not changing, you are choosing." There is power in your words—are you going to speak death or life over your situation?

We all face different seasons in life, but how we act and react during those seasons is what God wants us to learn. He wants to strengthen us. He wants us to trust Him and have faith in Him. Negative thoughts will only bring fear and keep us from claiming victory.

Fear works like faith, but in the opposite direction. Both ask us to believe in something that we cannot see. The enemy wants us stuck, scared, and stagnant. I am sure Joshua was afraid, but he did not let those giant walls stop him. God gave him a Word, a plan specific to his current need; and Joshua was determined not to let fear win.

> Fear works like faith... in the Opposite direction.

To carry out God's plan, the army was arranged carefully: armed guards first, followed by the priests carrying the Ark of the Covenant. Seven priests blowing trumpets marched in front of the Ark. Then came more soldiers and the rest of the Israelites. Every detail of God's plan served a purpose, even when it didn't make sense to human reasoning.

For instance, the army was to march around the city once a day for six days in total silence; only the trumpets could blow. On the seventh day, they were to march around the city seven times with the priests blowing the trumpets. When they heard a long blast, the entire army was to give a shout. I find it very

> Faith gives God room to Move

interesting that God commanded the army to be quiet as they were marching around the city every day. They were not to say a word.

Why do you think God told them to stay silent? I can't help but wonder if He was thinking, "I do not need anyone speaking negative words and complaining." Murmuring gives the enemy room to work, but faith gives God room to move. I am sure the Israelites were thinking, "How in the world is walking around this city without saying a word going to change anything? How is this benefiting me at all?" It sounded crazy and felt ridiculous.

God had a plan, and His plans are always good. He was trying to get something to them; not just a victory, but deeper faith. God knew negative words would spread like wildfire, so He commanded silence. It would have taken just one complaint to unravel the courage they needed. Your words are powerful.

Faith means trusting when it doesn't make sense. Marching silently around a wall felt ridiculous. Standing so close to the Promised Land, yet facing an impossible barrier, must have been heartbreaking. But God was writing a bigger story—one that required obedience before they could see the outcome.

Think about what might separate you from your miracle today. What wall stands towering over you, daring you to quit? Maybe you feel like turning back, giving up, and returning to the comfort of what's familiar. But hear me—you are too close now. The breakthrough is just ahead. Don't let fear talk you out of it.

God commanded the army to walk around the massive city walls once a day for six days—in total silence. No talking, no murmuring, not even a whisper. Then, on the seventh day, they were to march around it seven times and on the seventh time, they were to lift their voices in a mighty shout. It must have sounded crazy, absurd even, but they obeyed. Sometimes obedience looks crazy before it looks victorious.

> God is working behind the Scenes

As they circled the city one last time, I imagine hope pounding in their chests. Every lap was a step of faith, and now they were on the brink of their breakthrough. They trusted God's Word without seeing a single crack in the walls and then, on the seventh day, on the seventh lap, it happened. *"By faith the walls of Jericho fell after they were encircled for seven days"* (Hebrews 11:30, NKJV). With one mighty shout of obedience, the walls crumbled beneath them.

Maybe you are circling your own wall today, feeling like nothing is changing. But God is still working. He calls you to look past what you see with your eyes and hold on to what He has promised. His ways are higher, His strength is greater, and His provision is already on the way.

As the Israelites marched, nothing seemed to change. No cracks formed, the stones did not shift, yet they kept moving. Faith doesn't wait for visible signs; it keeps walking, trusting God is working behind the scenes. Even when it looks hopeless, even when it feels impossible—keep marching. Your breakthrough is closer than you think.

Every lap around your giant wall strengthens your faith. Every prayer, every praise strengthens your faith muscles. God could have flattened Jericho instantly, but sometimes, the process prepares you for the promise. God wants your eyes on Him and not on the size of your wall.

Many times, we allow our circumstances to grow because we fail to take our thoughts captive. Fear plants a seed, and if we don't address it, it grows into something overwhelming, just like the snake in my bathroom. What started as a minor problem became a life-threatening monster in my mind. How quickly fear distorts reality when we forget who is standing just outside the door, ready to protect us.

But don't we often do the same when we are facing real-life problems that feel too big to handle? We forget to pause, to breathe, and remember that our Heavenly Father stands beside us. He promises to *never leave us nor forsake us,* but when fear creeps in, it distorts our view. The walls seem taller. The battle feels too great. When we let fear go unchecked, instead of magnifying God, we magnify the problem and slowly, our peace slips away.

Too often, we let disappointment take root, and we replay the doctor's words over and over until we are overwhelmed with fear and doubt. In seasons where you are walking around walls that feel impossible to break down, you face a choice: will you focus on the size of the wall or the greatness of your God? God is the God of the impossible. No matter how big the wall, how long the wait, or how fierce the battle seems, He is bigger. He is faithful. We have to learn to magnify Him more than we magnify what's standing against us. I know it feels hard sometimes. I know it feels impossible. But hear me, you are closer than you think.

> No matter how Big the wall... He is bigger

I have heard it said, "Just before your greatest victory, you will encounter your biggest obstacle." The Israelites were on the brink of entering their Promised Land—something they had waited a long time for. But right before their promise was fulfilled, a giant city stood in their way. In the natural, it seemed too big to conquer, but we serve a miracle-working God. No matter what you are up against today, I want you to know: God already has it under control. He's not asking for your fear or your frustration. He's asking for your trust. Your obedience to trust is the key that unlocks the door to your breakthrough.

When we trust in the Lord, we stop trying to figure it out ourselves. We learn to rest in the truth that He sees what we cannot see, and He understands what we cannot understand. Trust calls us to praise *before* we see the victory, not just after. Praising God after the walls fall, is celebration; praising Him while the walls are still standing—that is faith.

I believe the opposite of faith is not fear; it's control. When we try to manage everything ourselves instead of surrendering to God's timing, we only wear ourselves down with anxiety and doubt. It is natural to want to fix things. Mamas want to fix boo-boos, and daddies want to fix tough situations, but some battles aren't ours to fix. God needs us to let go and trust Him—even when we do not understand. We cannot hold on to control and still walk in true joy. His plan is always better, and always worth trusting. Even when fear tempts us to speak defeat, we must resist it. Fear doesn't move mountains; faith does.

When you face a mountain, you have a decision to make: will you keep striving in your own strength, or will you trust God enough to speak to that mountain in faith? Mark 11:23 says, *"For assuredly, I say to you, whoever says to this mountain, 'Be removed and be cast into the sea,' and does not doubt in his heart, but believes that those things he says will be done, he will have whatever he says"* (NKJV). Your words carry power, so what are you speaking to your mountain?

> Praise pushes you into your Victory

Learn to praise before the victory. Faith releases God's hands to move; fear only strengthens the enemy's hold. If you give up now, you risk staying stuck in circles of defeat, regret, and bitterness. Remember, praise isn't reserved for *when* the walls fall—it's the very thing that brings them down.

Your praise pushes you into your victory. It declares, "I have not seen it yet, but I believe it will happen." That kind of faith moves the heart of God. Imagine if Joshua and his army had stopped on the sixth lap around Jericho? They would have been right on the edge of their promise, yet walked away. What if you're just one shout away from your breakthrough today? I know it feels overwhelming, but you are closer than you think.

We need to be careful about letting our thoughts run away from us. That is exactly what happened in my snake-in-the-bathroom story. It might sound silly, but in that moment, I truly believed that snake was going to eat me. The longer I stared at what I thought was a five-foot monster, the more powerless I felt. And that's what fear does: it magnifies what isn't real until it steals our peace.

Be careful what you are speaking over your circumstances. Your words carry power. Are you speaking death over your problem, or are you speaking life? That choice is yours. Jesus said He *"came for us to have life, and have it more abundantly."* You could be one shout away from your victory. Don't let the enemy rob you of what God has promised. I believe something is stirring in your spirit even now. As you read these words, I believe your faith is rising. Stay faithful, and never forget how deeply He loves you.

In the moments when it feels hardest to stay grounded in the Word and speak His truth, it's easy to wonder, *"Does God even hear me?"* Let me reassure you: yes, God hears you. He always hears when you pray.

> When you walk by faith, walls fall, mountains move, and breakthroughs come.

So, keep marching, keep moving, and keep declaring His truth. Stop speaking doubt over the promises God is trying to bring into your life. Declare God's Word to your mountain. When you begin to walk by faith, not by sight, walls fall, mountains move, and breakthroughs come. Let God take control of your situation, and allow Him to fight your battles for you.

CHAPTER 3

THE BATTLE IS GOD'S, NOT YOURS

Not long after I found out about the diagnosis, a woman from church walked up to me one Sunday with a small gift bag in her hands. She said she had been shopping when she saw something that made her think of me. When I opened it, there was a beautiful plaque that simply read, "*The battle is God's, not yours.*" I stared at it for a long moment, reading it again and again, with tears welling in my eyes. I simply looked up at her and said, "Thank you." It was exactly what I needed at that moment.

God always sends reminders, I like to call "God Winks," to let us know He's near and that He's got it all under control. But if we're not careful, we miss them. Complaints, old hurts, and daily distractions pull our focus off His promises and onto our problems.

I have tried to make it a daily habit to thank God for the little things, which, when you really think about it, are actually the big things. It's amazing how changing your perspective changes everything. Now, I notice the sky's brilliance and the warmth of the sun on my face. Before, I might have missed it, or worse,

I may have complained about how hot it was (Florida summers will do that to you!), but now, during my morning walks, I find myself saying, "Wow, the sky sure is beautiful." Today, I choose to praise. I praise Him for both the big and the small. What I once overlooked now comes alive with His goodness.

God has surely given me a new lease on life. I don't take any of it for granted anymore. Do I mess up some days? Absolutely. I get it wrong more often than I'd like, but His grace and mercy remind me, I don't have to be perfect because He is. Maybe you need to hear that today: you are not perfect, and you will make mistakes, but God still loves you and His grace covers you.

Tomorrow is a new day. His mercies are new every morning. As it says in Lamentations, *"Through the Lord's mercies we are not consumed, Because His compassions fail not. They are new every morning; Great is Your faithfulness"* (Lamentations 3:22-23, NKJV). That is good news for us because no matter what you face, God's compassion never fails, and His faithfulness never ends.

I would define myself as a grateful person overall, but after you go through some things, it changes you. Now, I look for things to thank the Lord daily. It's easy to focus on problems and pain, but the easy road isn't always the best one. I am learning that it is possible to find joy even in the middle of pain.

One morning on my walk, I felt God was speaking to my heart. I always prayed during these walks, but that day I didn't even have the strength to pray. Have you ever had one of those days—a day that's just heavy, lonely, where you can't even find the words? That was me. I felt exhausted, overwhelmed, and I let the dark thoughts creep in.

I walked with my head down and stared at my shoes the whole time, never really looking up. I didn't smile at the people passing by, I didn't lift my eyes to meet theirs. All I could think about was how long this walk felt. I just wanted to get home, sit in my cool house and feel sorry for myself.

> What you focus on will always be magnified.

But in that quiet heaviness, I heard God whisper to my heart, *"As long as you keep looking down, you will not see the beauty that's all around."*

When I looked down, I was only focused on my problems. But I felt God say, *"Look up and keep looking up,"* and in that moment, something shifted in me. As I lifted my head, I saw the beauty that was all around. The sky was bluer, the trees were greener, and the birds were singing so beautifully. Beauty was all around me, but I hadn't noticed before because I was looking down.

What was I doing? My eyes were fixed on my problems, but when I lifted my head, everything shifted. I got my eyes off my problems and onto my God. He was trying to show me the bigger picture, if only I would stop looking down, feeling sorry for myself.

What you focus on will always be magnified. If you focus on how big your problems are, they will feel even bigger. They will overwhelm you, and everything you see will feel tainted by defeat. But what would happen if, instead of magnifying our problems, we started magnifying our God in the midst of them?

In the Bible, there was a good king of Judah named Jehoshaphat, who sought God's direction for his people. One day, his leaders came to him with terrifying news and said, *"A big army is coming for us."* It was not just one army; there were multiple armies coming against him (2 Chronicles 20:2, NKJV).

What do you do when you face an unexpected battle? When people and circumstances surround you, and it is hard to catch your breath. That's exactly where Jehoshaphat found himself. This was not just an attack on his army—it was personal. The enemy wanted to destroy him, to steal his hope, and to keep his eyes off of God. Likewise, he wants to make your life miserable and will continue to kick you while you are down. He wants to destroy you and keep your focus off of God.

I love what Jehoshaphat did next. Though afraid, he didn't panic or run away. Instead, he gathered the people and called them to seek the Lord through prayer and fasting. We need the Lord's help, because we can't fight our battles alone.

Scripture is clear: Jehoshaphat was afraid. Fear in itself isn't the problem—it's how we respond to it that matters most. What will your response be when you face an unexpected battle and fear threatens to consume you?

> God is in the battle-fighting business.

We need the Lord to help us, because we can't do it ourselves. Your initial response should always be to turn to God in spite of the fear, because that decision sets you up for the victory to come.

God is in the battle-fighting business. Nothing is too big or too scary for Him. He sees it all and knows it all. Yet, so often, we still try to fight our battles ourselves. I believe the Lord is saying to you right now, "*I want My battle back. That's My battle you are exhausting yourself trying to win. That is My battle keeping you up at night, searching for answers. Give Me back My battle.*"

So, what should you do in those first moments of a hard season? Pray. Prayer should be your first response, not your last resort. When the messengers came to King Jehoshaphat, his response was quick, simple, and direct: "*We are taking it to the Lord in prayer and fasting*" (2nd Chronicles 20:3-4, NKJV). Many times, we overthink it and run to others for advice. We don't need to ask others what we need to do—we need to ask God. Your friends on social media do not know the answer, and just because they are your "friends" on these social media platforms, does not qualify them to speak into your life.

Jehoshaphat didn't run to his leaders for counsel. He went immediately to the Lord. He was shocked by the unexpected battle, but he was not shaken. Scripture is clear that he was afraid—and it is okay for you to be afraid too. But be afraid and then take it to the Lord. Don't stay stuck in fear. If you let fear fester, it will grow into something very ugly.

Then Jehoshaphat prayed. I love reading his prayer because it reminds us to remember. Do not forget to remember what God has already done for you. He was faithful then, and He will be faithful now. In his prayer, he says, "*Are You not God in Heaven,*

> We do not know what to do, but our Eyes are upon You.

and do you not rule over all the kingdoms of the nations, and in Your hand is there not power and might, so that no one is able to withstand You?" (2 Chronicles 20:6, NKJV). What was he doing? He was speaking faith and declaring the future based upon what God had already done. He remembered that God was with him before, and this battle would be no different.

The very last verse of his prayer reads: *"We do not know what to do, but our eyes are upon You."* (2 Chronicles 20:12, NKJV). That is exactly where I want to be when hard times hit. Life sometimes blindsides us, and we wonder, "How did it get to this point?" But prayers like this make all the difference. We don't always know what to do, but we know a God who does.

After Jehoshaphat prayed, a prophet came with a word from the Lord: *"You will not need to fight in this battle. Position yourselves, stand still and see the salvation of the Lord, who is with you, O Judah and Jerusalem! Do not fear or be dismayed; tomorrow go out against them, for the Lord is with you"* (2 Chronicles 20:17, NKJV). In the middle of what seemed hopeless, God showed up. He will show up for you too.

That scripture has carried me through so many battles. I have even highlighted it in my Bible as a daily reminder. Maybe you are reading this and thinking, "I am in a big battle right now, and I don't know what to do." Don't fear, there is hope in Jesus.

He will fight this battle for you. And I believe the Lord is saying to you right now, *"He wants His battle back. You are fighting a battle He never asked you to fight."*

King Jehoshaphat heard from the Lord. He was still afraid, but he trusted God to fight for him. He did not know exactly how it would work out, but he had a promise to hold onto: God had done it before, and He would do it again. Somebody needs to hear that today: *If God has worked a miracle in your life once, He will not abandon you now. His promise still stands. He will do it again.*

> You are fighting a battle He never asked you to fight.

Even in fear, the king obeyed. The Lord said: *"Stand firm and position yourselves"* (2nd Chronicles 20:17, NKJV). According to Webster's Dictionary, to stand firm means "to refuse to change your decision or position." We often hear from God, but forget His Word as soon as life gets hard. We get confused, scared, and end up back at square one. But Jehoshaphat did not make that mistake. He and his army set out early the next morning.

Then, King Jehoshaphat did something so unusual: he placed the "praisers" at the front of the army. Can you imagine? An entire army marching out, and leading the way was not the soldiers but the choir. I wonder if the men thought, *"What in the world is the king doing?"* It made no military sense. But it made perfect God-sense. I want to remind you today; *your praise is a weapon.* Your shout confuses the enemy. The battle you are facing may be hard, but when you give it to God and let Him fight for you, it will take your faith to a whole new level. As the worshipers sang, *"Praise the Lord, for His mercy endures forever"* (2 Chronicles 20:21, NKJV), something powerful happened.

As they marched forward, the Lord began to set ambushes against the three other armies. The enemy was confused, and they began destroying each other. By the time Judah's army reached the battlefield, all they saw were dead bodies. God fought the battle for them. The best part of this story is that they never even had to fight.

> ...*you are about to find your strength*

God will fight your battle for you too. But we have to trust, obey, and praise before you see the outcome. Many people wait until the promise is fulfilled to praise. However, that is not faith. *Faith is praising Him before you see it.* Are you praising Him before the bill is paid? Before the marriage is restored? Before the healing comes? It would have been easier for Jehoshaphat if God had just told him exactly how it would unfold. But that is not how faith works. And it would be nice if God told us the details of our lives, too. But He calls us to trust Him even when we do not understand.

You may be in a battle right now, but because of your struggle, you are about to find your strength. Remember, God wants to fight this battle for you—but you have to let Him. You have been trying to force puzzle pieces together that do not fit, and it's leaving you tired and frustrated. God is asking you for every piece of the puzzle, not just the ones you're willing to let go of.

I'm reminded of when my kids were little, and we would do puzzles together as a family. We would spend an hour working on a puzzle, only to realize that a piece or two was missing. My daughter would look under the table, only to find after searching everywhere that her brothers, James and Joshua, had hidden the last few puzzle pieces under their legs. They said they wanted to be the ones to finish the puzzle.

I wonder, how often do we do the same with God? We hold on to the final pieces of the puzzle because we want to remain in control.

Maybe it's fear.

Maybe it's doubt.

Maybe it's pride.

But here's the truth: you cannot complete the puzzle unless you surrender every piece. You expect God to "fix it," but you're still holding the missing pieces. You try to jam broken pieces together and wonder why it doesn't fit. But when you fully surrender, God takes those scattered pieces and makes a masterpiece.

God sees the big picture. He sees the end from the beginning (Isaiah 46:10) and when you trust Him, you will see that He is faithful. Only God could cause three giant armies to destroy each other before Judah arrived. But it only happened after the king demonstrated his trust in God through his obedience, not before. I am sure that is not how King Jehoshaphat imagined the victory would come. God's plan often looks very different than ours, but it is always better.

You may be going through a hard time right now, but this is just a *season*.

> The battle is God's not yours

It is not a forever season—it is a season of trusting, waiting, and declaring God's faithfulness. He will work it out in His perfect timing. His promises are true every day. I will leave you with the same words, written on that plaque that still hangs in my home today: *"The battle is God's, not yours."*

CHAPTER 4

FEAR IS A LIAR

This morning, as I sit writing this chapter, I'm sipping the coffee my husband sweetly brought to me in a mug that reads: "Faith Before Fear." I love seeing those words, especially first thing in the morning. It sets the tone for my day, reminding me to trust in God, no matter what lies ahead. It reminds me that He is in control. Fear can take hold if we allow it, which is why it's so important to take control of it immediately. I once heard someone say, "If you do not take control of fear, it will take control of you."

Do you remember that old TV show where the contestants were challenged to conquer their fears? They faced terrifying stunts—wading through snakes, being trapped with bugs, or eating truly disgusting things. Sometimes, it was so intense, I could hardly watch! These contestants had to decide if they had the determination to face their fears. But, if they finished the challenges, they would win a cash prize. It was a true mind-over-matter experience.

It made me think: what do we have to do to overcome fear? Some people fear snakes, heights, the dentist, or public speaking. Would you do something like that show to help overcome your fear? What about the fear that keeps us from becoming everything God has called us to be?

This was certainly true for me when my husband and I were first called into the ministry. Jamie and I gave our lives to Jesus about a year after we were married, and not long after, we felt the call to help out with our church's youth group. The following summer, the group planned a mission trip to Venezuela. We desperately wanted to go, but could not afford it.

That's when an elderly couple approached us, saying they felt led by the Lord to pay for our trip. Their generosity floored us. We were shocked, excited, and scared all at once. We had never even been out of the state, let alone the country. On that trip, we experienced God's presence in ways we had never seen before. We witnessed healings and miracles. It was all so new to me. I hadn't grown up in church. My church experience was limited to an occasional visit with my aunt—but this? This was a whole new world. God was revealing things that would forever change my life.

I remember one night when they asked Jamie to share his testimony before the church. I was nervous for him, but even more proud. As I watched him speak, I saw a confidence rise in him that I had never seen before. As the week went on, we both sensed the Lord stirring something deeper. It was on this trip that Jamie looked at me and said, "I think God is calling us into the ministry." I felt it too and said, "Let's do it."

When we returned home from Venezuela, the reality of ministry work started sinking in. *What had I just agreed to?* I knew I had felt the same calling Jamie did, but suddenly, doubt crept in. I asked Jamie if he still felt called into ministry. "Yes," he said without hesitation. And I wondered, *did God change His mind about me? Or was I letting fear stop me?*

> Did God Change His mind about me?

I started giving God every excuse in the book: "I didn't grow up in church." "I don't know the Bible well enough." "I'm way too shy." And my personal favorite: "I can't even play the piano." Yes, I reminded God that I couldn't play the piano.

You see, my pastor's wife could preach and play the piano. In my mind, that became my image of what ministry was supposed to look like. I thought, "*If I could be like her, then I could do anything.*" It's crazy what we can convince ourselves of, isn't it? I even asked her to teach me how to play the piano. After years of lessons, I finally realized it just wasn't for me.

Eventually, I opened up to her about my fears. I was terrified of failing God. I was trapped in the comparison game, convinced that if I couldn't be like her, I wasn't qualified. She listened patiently, encouraged me, and shared her own fears when she was starting out. She reminded me that God does not ask us to be someone else—He asks us to be obedient.

I began to pray daily, asking God to help me release my fears. Truthfully, they still creep in from time to time. But I had to make a decision: Would I

> ...He would bring me through it.

let fear stop me from stepping into God's plan, or would I move forward anyway? I believe what you don't change, you are choosing. Even though the thought of ministry terrified me, I did not want to live a life controlled by fear. If my God brought me to it, He would bring me through it.

As of right now, we are in our thirty-third year of ministry. There have been a lot of ups and downs, but God has remained faithful through it all. I have a lot of ministry years behind me now, and I have learned so much along the way. There were many times the enemy would whisper, *"What are you doing here? You are not making a difference."* But I learned to lean on the Lord—especially when I felt afraid.

Many times, I think it is actually good to feel a little scared when you're stepping into what God has called you to do. Why? Because it makes you lean into Him even more. It forces you to trust Him instead of trusting in your own strength.

Have you been letting fear take control of your life? I want to encourage you today: You have control over what tries to control you. Through Jesus, you have the authority to say, *"Enough is enough!"* God has so much for you, and He has it all figured out.

Fear is the greatest weapon the enemy uses against us. It keeps us down, distracted, and crippled, which prevents us from being everything God created us to be. 2 Timothy 1:7 reminds us of the truth: *"For God has not given us a spirit of fear, but of power and of love and of a sound mind."* (NKJV).

From this verse, we know two powerful things: First, fear does not come from God—it comes from the enemy. Secondly, fear is outnumbered three to one! God has given us power, love, and a sound mind to overcome anything fear tries to say. God has given us power through Jesus to take what the enemy meant for harm and place it into God's hands.

He's given us His unfailing love, even when we didn't deserve it. And He's given us a sound mind—a mind that is firm and stable in Him. There are plenty of days I don't feel like my mind is stable, but through God's power, I can stand strong. We have everything we need to overcome what the enemy throws at us. And we must remember, fear has no rightful place in our hearts or minds.

If we are not careful, fear will try to control our lives. When we act out of fear, it causes us to do things we would not normally do. It's okay to be fearful at times, but where it becomes dangerous is when we allow fear to define us. Fear lies. It stirs emotions that cloud reason, pushing us to react rather than respond with faith. Fear has no rightful place in our lives, but if left unchecked, it will try to creep in and settle.

It was one thing to battle fear when stepping into ministry, but it was an entirely different level of fear when I was diagnosed with breast cancer. There were many days I fought just to get out of bed. The days I had to go to my appointments and chemotherapy felt very overwhelming. Fighting fear became a daily decision—especially in the beginning.

> It's okay to be fearful at times...

The enemy flooded my mind with lies, whispering worst-case scenarios. No one expects the word "cancer" to become a part of their story. Yet there I was, facing a road I never imagined I would walk. The journey ahead looked hard and painful, but deep down, I believed it would make me stronger. I had to find my brave. I had to choose: *Would I let this make me better or bitter?*

I remember Jamie printing out scripture verses and taping them all over our home. They were in the bathroom, the bedroom—even the car. I needed truth constantly in front of me. There were twists and turns during that journey that shook me to my core, but seeing God's Word every step of the way anchored my heart. It was a lifeline when fear tried to take over again.

It was really hard after each oncologist appointment. As I have said before, walking into the cancer center felt like walking into a heavy cloud of sorrow. People were hurting everywhere you looked. You could feel the weight of it pressing down. It was heartbreaking to see, and I had to give myself extra grace on those days.

After every appointment, I had to remind myself of God's promise: *"I shall not die, but live, and declare the works of the Lord"* (Psalm 118:17, NKJV). I constantly repeated that verse. If I ever stopped declaring the truth, the weight of fear would try to wrap itself around me again. I had to take authority over it or it would have taken authority over me.

I will never forget my first radiologist appointment. The room was large, cold, and intimidating. The radiologist carefully positioned me on the table. The tumor was on my left side, which meant they had to be extremely cautious near my heart. The doctor explained the procedure, asked me to stay perfectly still, and then he left the room as the radiation began. There I was, lying on the cold table, in a huge room all alone; I was absolutely terrified.

It felt like I was lying on that table for an hour, but in reality, it was only a few minutes. As the door closed behind the doctor, I whispered in my heart, *"God, You will never walk out on me."* In that cold, terrifying moment, I prayed and thanked God for staying with me through one of the most fearful times of my life. From that day forward, at every radiology appointment, I repeated the same declaration: *"God, I am not in this room alone—You are here with me. You have me close to You right now."*

I want to remind someone reading today: You are not alone. Fear may have gripped your heart, but you do not have to stay bound by it. The Bible speaks directly to this truth: *"Fear not, for I am with you; Be not dismayed, for I am your God. I will strengthen you, yes, I will help you, I will uphold you with My righteous right hand"* (Isaiah 41:10, NKJV).

> "God, You will never walk out on me."

If your kids are not serving the Lord—He is with you.

If your boss tells you that you are no longer needed—He is with you.

If the doctor delivers hard news—He is with you.

If divorce papers land in your hands—He is with you.

No matter what comes your way—He is with you.

> Fear is a stronghold...Keeping us bound.

Fear may try to steal your joy, but remember: *"The joy of the Lord is your strength"* (Nehemiah 8:10, NKJV). That strength that He gives will carry you through this season.

We have a choice every day: to speak fear or faith. What are you letting into your mind? The problem is not being afraid—fear is a human response. The real danger is when we allow fear to settle and make a home in our thoughts. If we allow it to linger, fear grows, takes root, and eventually tries to rule our lives. Fear is a stronghold that loves to wrap its ugly arms around our hearts and minds, keeping us bound.

Fear whispers *"You're never going to make it."*
Fear says, *"You're going to die,"*
Fear shouts, *"No one loves you."*
But every one of these voices is a lie from the enemy.

When we rehearse lies in our minds, they become the lens through which we see our lives and they keep us from reaching the promises God has for us. You cannot think, "I am a loser," and expect to live like more than a conqueror. Fear will take you down a road you never intended to travel if you allow it to settle. You have to remember: *fear is a liar.*

If the enemy's greatest weapon is lying, then our greatest weapon is the unchanging truth of God. God's truth never bends to circumstances. His Word doesn't shift based on how heavy the storm feels. Your feelings may change from day to day, but His truth remains constant, and His truth will set you free

(John 8:32 NKJV). His Word will set you free from the lies, it will free you from addiction, and it will free you from fear. Truth is not just informational—it's transformational. It is your weapon against every whisper of defeat the enemy tries to send your way.

There is someone reading this right now who needs a reminder:

You are not who fear says you are.

You are not your mistakes.

You are not your past.

These labels do not define you. They never did. Let God speak over your identity. In Christ, you are an overcomer.

Your life may have taken some twists and turns. You may feel defeated, let down, and convinced that fear has won, but listen to what Jesus says in John 16:33 (NKJV): *"These things I have spoken to you, that in Me you may have peace. In the world you will have tribulation; but be of good cheer, I have overcome the world."*

> He has overcome the world…

That is great news, my friend! He has overcome the world, and that includes your sickness, your depression, your anxiety, your broken past and your fear. In this world, you will face hard things, but you can anchor your soul in the truth that His promises are still "Yes" and "Amen" (2 Corinthians 1:20, NKJV).

You are not a product of your failures.

You are not the cruel words spoken over you.

You are not defined by your worst moment.

You are who God says you are.

God says you are redeemed, loved, and called according to His purpose. (Jeremiah 29:11, paraphrased)

You may be thinking, "What I'm going through right now is bringing so much fear into my life—how can I get past it?" The answer is simple to give, but often harder to do: you have to give your fears to God.

You cannot always control what happens to you, but you can control how you respond. When you are living in a constant state of worry, fear, and anxiety, it begins to spiral out of control. Sometimes, that means it's time to distance yourself from negative influences. Maybe it is time to take a break from social media, or maybe it's time to step away from voices that feed your fear instead of building your faith. What you allow into your mind has the power to shape your life.

Fear can be a human response, but we cannot stay there. We are not called to live in a spirit of fear; we are called to walk in the spirit of power, love, and a sound mind. If you feel stuck today, take heart— God is with you. He promises to help you through whatever you are facing. He is always speaking, but are you listening?

Whatever fear you are staring down right now may seem huge, but your God is so much bigger. He is stronger. He is faithful. You may feel overwhelmed at this moment, but remember, you serve the One who has never lost a battle.

I now understand fully that fear is a liar. It rears its ugly head and tries to take me down, but I am an overcomer. The words I speak and the thoughts I have matter. What are you speaking over your life?

Are you speaking fear, or are you speaking faith? Many times, in our lives, we stay stuck in neutral because we are paralyzed by fear of what the future might hold. But God has a future for you—a future that is not ruled by fear; it is a future full of hope.

As we continue to the next chapter, I want to focus on what we are telling our minds. Sometimes, we need to slow down and *"think about what we're thinking about."* Controlling your thoughts starts with recognizing how much they matter. It's true: what fills your mind, fills your life.

CHAPTER 5

STOP PLAYING MIND GAMES

Have you ever played the game "*Two Truths and a Lie*"? In this game, you share three statements about yourself. Two of the statements are true and one is false. As youth pastors, we used to play it all the time. It was one of the best icebreakers, especially when people didn't know each other well.

It was always hilarious to hear the lies people came up with. The key was to make the lie believable, so you couldn't say, "*I have a million dollars in my bank account.*" (Who has that these days?) If it's too obvious, everyone will guess right away. The best lies were the ones that sounded mostly true with just one little twist.

I think sometimes we play a version of this game in real life. If we are not careful, we start believing the lies we tell ourselves. It comes down to the truth of God's Word versus the lies of the enemy.

> The enemy loves to twist the Word of God...

We have to ask ourselves: *Which one are we going to believe?* If you believe a lie long enough, it can become your truth. We might say one thing, but deep down believe something entirely different.

The enemy loves to twist the Word of God just enough to make it sound believable. If we do not know the truth of God's Word, it's easy to slip into doubt, fear, and deception. That's exactly where the enemy wants us—bound, fearful, and stuck. 1 Peter 5:8 warns us, *"Be sober, be vigilant; because your adversary the devil walks about like a roaring lion, seeking whom he may devour"* (NKJV).

My grandson Judah loves animals. If you show him a picture of any animal, not only can he name it, but he'll also tell you what it eats, where it lives, and even some fun facts. The lion ranks in his top five favorites. One Christmas, he and his little brother Benaiah gave me a toy lion. Judah said with a big smile,

> *"Gigi, this is my favorite animal. Now it's your favorite animal too."*

I laughed and said,

> *"Of course it is, buddy. How did you know?"*

I've picked up a lot about animals over the years. First from my boys, Joshua and James, and now from the grandkids. Apparently, it runs in the family! Lions are amazing creatures. Interestingly, it's usually the lionesses who do the hunting, while the male lions stay back to guard the pride's territory.

A lion's roar is powerful. It can be heard up to five miles away, and can reach a deafening 114 decibels, which is louder than a chainsaw. When the lion roars, he rises to his full height and changes his stance. It's his way of declaring, *"I'm the king here. Stay back."* He is always alert, listening carefully for signs of danger.

What are you listening to in your life? There is so much noise all around us. We have noise from the television, from social media, and from the culture around us. However, we have to discern whether it is the Lord, the whisper of the enemy, or our own flesh.

Scripture warns us that the enemy prowls around like a roaring lion. He tries to imitate something he will never truly be. The enemy may try to roar loudly to intimidate us, but the truth is, he has no real power over us. He tries to sound fierce, but he is not a lion—and he never will be.

> ...the truth is, he has no real *power* over us.

We must know the difference between the imitation and the real thing. Jesus is the real Lion—the Lion of Judah—and He came to give us life, and life more abundantly (John 10:10).

It's time for us to change our stance. Just like a lion, we need to rise up. For far too long, we've been sitting back and letting the enemy run all over us. It's time to stand firm, to claim what God has promised us, and to walk in the authority He has given us. You are a child of the Most High God—it's time to start living like it!

Too often, we find ourselves listening to the enemy's lies, which leave us bound by guilt, shame, or fear. When you study lions, you realize something powerful: lions are known for their strength, their beauty, and their fearlessness. They don't run from fear; they face it head-on with courage.

If a lion senses danger, he doesn't overthink it or second-guess himself. He acts boldly and decisively. Lions are naturally discerning; they can distinguish the difference between a leaf rustling in the wind and the sound of a leaf crushed underfoot by approaching danger. It is in their DNA. I believe we can learn something from that same fearless discernment.

We need to discern the truth from the lie. We need to recognize the difference between an imitator and the Great Lion of Judah. Lies can show up wrapped in a pretty package, but in the end, a lie is still a lie. In the midst of all the noise around us, we must tune our hearts to the still, small voice of the Lord. He is the One that we need to trust completely and without fear.

We spend so much energy trying to figure a way out of our problems that we forget the simplest truth: God is the way out. Instead of trusting Him, we stress, overthink, and exhaust ourselves trying to fix what only He can fix. Raise your hand if you've been there. I know I have.

God is calling us to live bravely and to remember who we are. During the cancer treatments, the Lord placed an idea on my heart to create what I now call "*Brave Boxes.*" These are small care packages meant to comfort others walking a similar road. They are filled with items that brought me comfort: a devotional, coffee mug, T-shirt, Scriptures, and notepad. And when you open up the box, right inside the lid it reads: "*Brave is not the absence of fear, but the courage to face it.*"

> *Brave is not the absence of fear, but the courage to face it.*

You can be scared and brave at the same time. That's why it's so important to take inventory of what goes on in your mind daily. I've said it before: "*Think about what you are thinking about.*" It may sound strange, but it's absolutely true.

So often, from the moment we get out of bed, until the moment we go back to sleep, we let negative thoughts run wild. Let's be honest— nobody wants to be around negativity 24/7. It's exhausting.

In her book, *Who Switched Off My Brain,* Dr. Caroline Leaf explains how to control our toxic thoughts and emotions (Leaf). She shares that "around 87% of illnesses can be attributed to our thought life, and approximately 13% to our diet, genetics, and environment" (Leaf). That's astounding! What we think about could literally be making us sick. Our minds are powerful tools that God created to speak either life or death into our situations; I emphasized this back in chapter 2.

Dr. Leaf also explains that fear is no small thing. It triggers more than 1,400 physical and chemical responses in your body (Leaf). It is not just a feeling—it is a whole-body experience (Leaf).

> You may not be able to control what happens to you...

Research also shows that "the average person has 12,000 to 50,000 thoughts per day. Of those thoughts, 80% are negative" (Leaf). When I first read that, it stunned me to see the impact of our thought life in our daily lives. It really makes you think, doesn't it?

My prayer for you as you read this book is simple: that you will start taking back control over your thoughts. You might be walking through a difficult season right now, but hear me—you already have everything you need to succeed. It is time to stop living a life driven by feelings or past failures. You may not be able to control what happens to you, but you absolutely have control over how you respond to it.

Romans 12:2 reminds us, *"And do not be conformed to this world, but be transformed by the renewing of your mind, that you may prove what is good and acceptable, and the perfect will of God"* (NKJV). Renewing your mind is not a one-time decision; it is a daily commitment. It means constantly seeking the Lord, staying rooted in prayer, and saturating yourself in His Word. It also means replacing every negative thought with the truth of God's promises. And after you do it today, you'll have to do it again tomorrow. It's a daily battle, but it is a battle worth fighting.

Just like the game I mentioned earlier, you have to replace the lie with the truth. When you find yourself facing a difficult situation, you have two choices: Will you believe the lie that says that you'll never make it, or are you going to believe the truth that says you are an overcomer? It's time to stop giving someone else the power to define your destiny.

> Take back what was stolen from you

It's time to take back what was stolen from you and rise up into the warrior God created you to be. It's time to take our thoughts back and align them with what God says. 2 Corinthians 10:5 says, *"Casting down arguments and every high thing that exalts itself against the knowledge of God, bringing every thought into captivity to the obedience of Christ"* (NKJV).

That means when a thought comes into your mind, you line it up with the Word of God. If it does not align, you take action. Through Jesus, you have the authority to stop those thoughts and bring them into obedience.

Have you ever had a headache and thought, *"Let me just Google this real quick"*—only to end up spiraling down a rabbit hole of terrifying diagnoses? What started as a small headache now has you convinced you have a brain tumor. Suddenly, Google is trying to kill you!

What happened? You opened your mind to everything the internet had to say without filtering it through God's truth. Fear grows when left unchecked. Small worries can escalate into full-blown panic if we don't guard our minds. Haven't we all been there at some point?

Don't let those thoughts take over. Don't give the enemy access. He can't read your mind, but he can whisper lies. Every time we speak negativity or entertain fear, we're giving him permission he doesn't deserve. Instead, take every thought captive and submit it to Christ.

A lot of the time, we like to blame everything on the devil. "The devil made me do it," or "The devil made me think it." Well, yes, the enemy plants thoughts in our minds, but more often than not, it's our own thinking that trips us up. We allow small, unchecked thoughts to settle, and before long, they grow into something much bigger than they ever should have been. Something that started out small now feels overwhelming. Ask yourself: What are you letting into your mind? What are you speaking over your family?

This is not about *"naming it and claiming it."* It's about obedience to God's Word. When a thought enters my mind, I've learned to immediately ask, *"Does this align with God's Word or with what God says about me?"* If it doesn't, I cast it down. Simple obedience, practiced daily, changes everything. We have the power to recognize the truth from the lie and choose what to believe.

What an amazing, merciful God we serve! He doesn't leave us guessing about how to win these mental battles. He gives us clear instructions: take every thought captive! It's hard sometimes, especially when life hits you with a doctor's report, financial struggles, or broken relationships, but we were never meant to fight alone. God is always with you, inviting you to hand over your thoughts, your fears, and your worries. You're never alone in the battle.

> God is Always with you...

Taking control of your mind is a process, and like anything worth mastering, it takes practice. It is like building a muscle—the more you train it, the stronger it becomes.

I still remember my daddy teaching me to drive his big old stick-shift truck. I was terrified behind that big steering wheel, but he would smile and say, *"Once you learn how to drive the stick shift, you will be able to drive anything."*

At first, every time I tried to shift gears, they would grind terribly. I'd get so frustrated I thought, *"Forget it! I'll just hitchhike everywhere!"* But my daddy wouldn't let me quit. He kept encouraging me: *"Let's try again."* I changed my thinking, pushed through the fear, and sure enough, after enough practice, I learned how to drive that big old truck.

The key to my success with learning to drive that truck was changing my *"stinkin' thinkin'"* and refusing to give up. When I thought I couldn't, I didn't. When I thought I could, I did. I may not have realized it at that time, but my thoughts were dictating my actions. I believed the lies in my head that said I would never learn. But thankfully, I had a daddy who didn't give up on me, and he pushed me to be better.

I want you to understand this too—you have a Father in Heaven, *who will never give up on you*. God sees what's inside you, even when you can't see it yourself. In Jeremiah 1:5 God says, *"Before I formed*

> *Your thoughts and words have the power...*

you in the womb, I knew you; before you were born, I sanctified you; I ordained you a prophet to the nations" (NKJV). How incredible it is to know that before you were ever even born, God set you apart and called you for a purpose! He said, *"I set you apart."*

So, when life gets heavy and hard, remember: *you are set apart.* You are called out of darkness, and God has given you everything you need to take your thoughts captive. If you think it can never happen, it likely won't.

Stop speaking death over your situation. Your thoughts and words have the power to bring either death or life over your situation. You get to choose.

If we are not careful, we'll try to take shortcuts to God. We will ask people to pray for us or recommend books to fix our thinking—and those things are wonderful tools, but at the end of the day, you have to do the hard work yourself. No one else can take control of your mind for you. God has already given you what you need inside of you, but you must stop playing mind games and start renewing your mind daily.

God's Spirit lives in you and empowers you to handle anything that may come your way. Taking your thoughts captive means you control them—not the other way around. Don't let the world's opinions, or even what the doctors may say, plant fear or negativity in your mind. I know how hard it can be to separate the truth from the noise.

It's a battle I fought daily during my journey with the diagnosis. If God helped me, He will help you. Some days I got it wrong, but I couldn't stay down. I had to keep getting back up and remind myself of God's truth: *"Weeping may last through the night, but joy comes in the morning"* (Psalm 30:5, NKJV). God will take the hard times you've walked through and will turn them into a beautiful testimony.

> God will take the hard times you've walked through...

CHAPTER 6

BEAUTY FROM ASHES

God can use the broken pieces of your life and turn them around for your good and His glory. I am living proof of that. There have been many times I doubted God could use my mess for anything, yet He still took a broken, shy, and insecure little girl and used her for things greater than she ever imagined.

I did not deserve it, but He did it anyway because that is who He is, and what He did for me, He will do for you too. He can take the hurts from your past and weave them into something beautiful for your future.

I am reminded of a story in the Bible of a king and an orphan girl named Esther. It's a story I love so much, I tell it often to my grandbabies. One Sunday after church, Ember, Sunnie, and Scarlett ran up to me with excitement.

"Gigi, guess what we talked about in class?" they said,

> *"Your favorite story—about Esther and how she was so brave."*

> ...*beautiful in His hands.*

I love how little ones are like little sponges, soaking in God's truth.

This story is a blend of betrayal, love, and redemption. It is a faithful reminder of the God we serve. I have often heard the saying: "God doesn't call the qualified, but He qualifies the called." And it's true. God specializes in taking the ashes we hold in our hands and transforming them into something beautiful in His hands.

In the book of Esther, we meet King Xerxes of Persia, who was married to Queen Vashti. The king, a wealthy and powerful man, threw a grand six-month-long party to show off his riches. It was lavish beyond imagination, with food, wine, and extravagance everywhere. But this king had a temper and an ego to match his wealth.

At the end of the party, King Xerxes summoned Queen Vashti to come before the guests. While the Bible doesn't specify exactly what he asked her to do, many believe he wanted her to parade herself in a degrading way. Whether that was true or not, Queen Vashti refused. She would not allow herself to be treated like a trophy. The king, humiliated and furious, banished her from the kingdom. And if anyone ever tells you the Bible is boring, just remind them of stories like this one—*it's anything but boring!*

He kicked her out of the kingdom. *Can you believe that*? Simply because she had the courage to say no to the craziness, she was banished! Yet, that's exactly what happened.

After Queen Vashti left, King Xerxes decided to find a new queen. His advisors spread out across Persia, gathering hundreds of young women to compete for the king's favor. It was essentially a giant beauty pageant to select the next queen. These young women underwent intense preparation, which included months of spa treatments, oils, and perfumes just for the chance at becoming queen.

The Bible describes the extensive beautification process in Esther 2:12: *"Each young woman's turn came to go in to King Ahasuerus after she had completed twelve months' preparation, according to the regulations for the women, for thus were the days of their preparation apportioned: six months with oil of myrrh, and six months with perfumes and preparations for beautifying women"* (NKJV). Can you even imagine twelve months of preparations? That's a lot of spa days!

This is where Esther enters the story. Esther was not only outwardly beautiful, but also kind-hearted and humble. She was a Jewish orphan, raised by her cousin Mordecai, who warned her to keep her Jewish heritage a secret while living in Persia. Esther agreed and went forward along with the other girls to meet the king.

Finally, when King Xerxes saw Esther, he knew immediately she was the one. Out of hundreds of women, Esther found favor in his eyes, and he chose her to be the new queen. I love that God took a young, orphaned Jewish girl—the most unlikely candidate—and placed her exactly where He needed her and exactly when He needed her. That is the kind of God we serve.

> He loves to take the broken, the overlooked, and the underqualified...

God still works like that today. He loves to take the broken, the overlooked, and the underqualified and uses them for His glory. In my own life, there were so many moments when I doubted God could ever use someone like me; times when I ignored what God asked me to do because I was scared or afraid of putting myself out there.

If I'm honest, my people-pleasing tendencies often got in the way of fully trusting God. But even then, time and time again, He has taken my broken pieces and turned them into something beautiful.

I remember many times trying to explain to God how I was not qualified to do what He was calling me to do. I told Him about all the broken pieces in my life, and how He surely couldn't use that for my good or for His glory. Fear and insecurity would get the best of me.

Maybe you have felt the same way too, thinking your mistakes or your past disqualified you from being used by God. The truth is, God is not looking for perfect people. Jesus is perfect, and because He is perfect, we do not have to be. By His grace and mercy, He gives us everything we need, and we can be assured that He's got our back.

> God can take something from nothing and make it beautiful

God can take something from nothing and make it beautiful. He can take our broken pieces and somehow put them back together in a way that brings strength and restoration to our lives. He is such a great God. All He needs is your willingness and your obedience.

King Xerxes and Queen Esther were married, and things seemed to be going well—until one day, Mordecai overheard a plot by a man named Haman. Haman was a wicked man who hated the Jews. He wanted Mordecai to bow to him, and Mordecai would not. So, Haman convinced the king to sign a decree to destroy all the Jews, not knowing that his new queen was also a Jew.

Mordecai went to Queen Esther and said, *"You have to do something to save your people."* Esther was terrified. Revealing her true identity could cost her everything, including her life. She stood at the crossroads, faced with one of the biggest decisions of her life. What should she do?

Mordecai reminded her that perhaps God placed her exactly where she was for this exact moment. Esther 4:14 says, *"For if you remain completely silent at this time, relief and deliverance will arise for the Jews from another place, but you and your father's house will perish. Yet who knows whether you have come to the kingdom for such a time as this?"* (NKJV). Esther realized she couldn't stay silent. She had to take a stand. Sometimes making the right decision is the hardest decision.

The queen would do the right thing even though it could cost her everything. Esther set a plan in motion, preparing a lavish banquet for the king and inviting Haman as well, thus creating an opportunity to expose Haman's evil plan. When the king saw all she had done, he told her he would grant her any request. This was her moment to tell the king everything that was going on—and hopefully have him spare her life.

With courage, she revealed her secret: "*I am a Jew, and someone is plotting to kill me and my people.*" Shocked, the king demanded to know who would dare such a thing. Esther pointed to Haman. The Bible says the king was furious. He ordered that Haman be hanged on the very gallows he had built for Mordecai.

> *I will never leave you nor forsake you.*

Each time I read the book of Esther; I am overwhelmed by the way God orchestrated every detail. Nothing was by accident. God placed Esther exactly where she needed to be *at exactly the right time*.

Just like that, God can turn things around in our lives in a split second. Esther had a tough decision to make, and it took incredible bravery and strength. Likewise, we will face obstacles in our lives where the situation seems impossible, but God always pulls us through. His Word reminds us, "*I will never leave you nor forsake you*" (Hebrews 13:5, NKJV).

You may be in a season right now that feels confusing or painful. You may be asking God, "*Why?*" or "*How long?*" as you're trying to make sense of it all. But hear me: there is always a reason for the season you are in. You may not see it yet, and you may not understand it in the moment, but you can trust that

God's plan is perfect. His ways are higher, and His timing is always best.

Whatever you are facing right now, remember: Jesus has already gone before you to make provision for every need. He knows there will be seasons of mourning, but He promises to turn your mourning into dancing. He knows there will be times when you feel buried in ashes, but He is the God who turns ashes into something beautiful.

> *Jesus has already gone before you...*

I believe God is reminding you today: *Don't stay stuck in the ashes*. Let Him redeem, restore, and bring you through the fire—without even the smell of smoke clinging to you.

You may have been knocked down, and you may have fallen many times, but God is saying, "*Get back up.*" This situation you are in will not overtake you. You are an overcomer, and your promise is waiting for you on the other side of this valley season. Nobody wants to walk through the valley, but it is in the valley where you are restored, healed, and refined.

To reach the mountaintop, you first have to pass through the valley. Your miracle is found in the valley, not on the mountaintop. The mountaintop simply reveals that the promise has already come to pass. It is easy to shout when you're standing in victory—but *can you shout while you're still in the valley*?

So, if you feel like you are in the valley today, keep praising and keep believing, because your promise is on the way. Your praise precedes your victory. You are going to fight, believe, and trust that God is making a way where there seems to be no way. He is already working on your behalf.

Just like the story of Esther, I believe God is raising you up right now—*for such a time as this.* This is not a time to shrink back or cower in fear. This is a time to rise up and boldly declare everything God has for you and your family. He is your provider. He is your healer. He is your restorer. He is the way-maker when there seems to be no way. He is everything you need and so much more.

Imagine if Esther had said, "*I can't be a queen because I'm just an orphan...and I am a Jew?*" I am sure people talked about her and put labels on her life: *She's an orphan.* Nobody wants her. How can she be the king's wife? How can she save an entire nation? I'm sure those thoughts ran through her mind too, but she didn't let those labels define her, and she didn't let them stop her.

Do not let the labels others have placed on you, or the labels you have placed on yourself, keep you from what God has called you to. God already knows your past—every mistake, every failure—and still He says, "*I choose you.*" What looks like defeat right now might just be God clearing the way for your promotion.

I am sure it looked hopeless for Esther. Telling the king the truth could have cost her everything. She had a decision to make, and I am sure she felt defeated, abandoned, lost, and hurt. But here's the key: she didn't let her past, or her fear, dictate her future.

I'll never forget one day walking into a gym and seeing a quote written in big, bold letters across the floor: "*Today's pain is tomorrow's strength.*" That simple phrase has stayed with me for years.

> Today's pain is tomorrow's strength.

The pain that you are facing today is building strength for your tomorrow. What God is doing in your life is bigger than anything you can see right now, and the enemy knows it too. That is why he tries so hard to make you feel defeated. He keeps pointing to the rubble and ashes you're standing in, but hear me—*he only wins if you let him*.

There were days when I looked in the mirror and saw the scars left from my breast cancer surgery and treatments. Every day, I remind myself: *My scars tell a story*. My scars remind me that I am a survivor—not marked by defeat, but by redemption. What once tried to kill me made me even stronger. *Your scars tell a story too*.

You are an unshakable force created by God "*for such a time as this.*" There is hope even in the midst of your hurt today. God will fight your battles—you simply need to hand them over to Him.

Where you are right now is not the final chapter of your story. The pages will turn, and you will overcome. The enemy may try to stop you, but your unshakable faith declares, "*No matter what comes my way, I will choose joy because the joy of the Lord is my strength*" (Nehemiah 8:10, NKJV).

Remember, there is purpose in your pain, and He is turning your ashes into something beautiful.

Although God did not give me cancer, He allowed it. And He has used the ashes for His glory. Because of yesterday's pain, I am now able to help people today—people who are walking through the unspeakable hurts that life can bring. *Today's pain is tomorrow's strength.*

I remember riding the elevator up with Jamie to a chemo appointment one day. A kind man and woman stepped into the elevator as well, and I could see the pain in her eyes. I could tell she was hurting. I felt a nudge from the Holy Spirit and asked if I could pray for her. We were strangers, just four people in an elevator, but in that moment, God was moving.

The second I asked, she broke down in tears. She told me she had thyroid cancer and was headed to a radiation appointment. She was terrified. Right there in the elevator, I spoke the name of Jesus over her and prayed for healing over her body. I declared boldly: *"The cancer is gone in Jesus' name."* Where did that boldness come from? It certainly wasn't from me—it was all Jesus.

> This is really not all about you.

Of course, there were other days when I didn't feel so bold. There were days when I prayed quietly, overwhelmed by the endless appointments and treatment plans. One day, in the midst of my frustration, I felt the Lord say, "*This is really not all about you.*" I can tell you—it sure felt like it was. I was the one having surgeries, losing my hair, and being sick and exhausted for months. All of this was happening to me.

But God gently whispered again, *"Yes, I'm doing something in you. But I'm also doing something in the people around you."* It wasn't just about me. It was about every person He would place in my path. That realization changed everything.

God was working through me to reach others. He still is. There are opportunities everywhere to reach those around us—if we just open our eyes to see them. People are hurting in hospitals, workplaces, cancer centers, even in the grocery store. They are waiting for someone to share the hope of Jesus with them.

I made a decision: I would not sit in my pain and wallow. I would let God use every part of my story for His glory. I finally understood that what He was doing through me was much bigger than me.

So, I made a vow that I would do everything I could for the glory of God. That is when my *Brave is Beautiful* boxes were born. As I shared in the previous chapter, these boxes are filled with hope for people walking through cancer, grief, or a hard season. Sometimes, when people are hurting, we want to help but don't know how. These boxes are a simple reminder for all who receive them: *Jesus has not given up on you.*

> Do not give up.
> Do not give in.
> You are worth it.

Had I not walked through the pain, I would not have walked into the victory. The path to victory is paved through perseverance—not giving up in your pain. I feel strongly that someone needs to hear this today: *Do not give up. Do not give in. You are worth it.* Jesus believed you were worth it so much that He died to prove it. Learning to find the joy in the middle of the pain has helped me survive many hard seasons, and it can help you too.

CHAPTER 7

JOY IN THE MIDDLE OF PAIN

One night, after showering, I went to brush my hair and a clump of hair came out. I stood there in shock, unwilling to believe it was really happening. Yet there I was, standing in the bathroom with a hairbrush in one hand and a clump of hair in the other. I remember looking in the mirror and telling God, *"I do not want to go through this."*

The doctors and nurses had warned me when to expect hair loss, but a part of me prayed I would be the exception—maybe it wouldn't happen to me. Maybe I would somehow keep my hair. Fear tried to take hold of me throughout the entire journey with breast cancer. And if I am honest, even now, years later, I still have to fight it—the fear of recurrence, the fear of leaving my husband, my children, and all my grandbabies too soon.

When you go through something like this, there is always a little crack that the enemy tries to creep into. He knows exactly where you struggle, and although he may try, he cannot win; *unless you let*

> The joy of the Lord is your strength.

him. Whenever fear tries to creep back in, I remind myself: God has the final word. I may have bad moments, even bad days, but I am still an overcomer. The enemy tried, but he never stole my joy.

After standing in the bathroom, holding that clump of my hair, I made a decision: I was going to take control of how I lost the rest. My hair had always been really long, flowing down my back. It was the one thing I was most anxious about losing. When you are fighting for your life, you do not really care about your hair, but walking through the process of losing it hit me harder than I ever expected.

My family threw me a "hair-cutting party," complete with good food and lots of laughter. A sweet friend came over to cut my hair really short, and she did an amazing job, but I'll never forget walking into the bathroom afterward, looking in the mirror, and bursting into tears. There was so much to process, and no matter how much I tried to brace myself, it still hit me hard—seeing all my long blonde hair almost completely gone. Even in that moment, the Lord gently whispered, *"The joy of the Lord is your strength."*

I did not feel strong standing there. I felt weak, small, and overwhelmed. But in that bathroom, God met me with words of hope. It was as if He spoke directly to my heart: *"You are weak, but with Me, you are made strong. You are going to make it through. Trust Me."*

If you feel weak right now, remember—you don't have to be strong on your own. His strength is more than enough for you. You do not have to go through this alone.

Being brave doesn't always feel like bravery. Bravery isn't a feeling—it is an action. It is taking one shaky step forward when you can't see where the road leads. Bravery is finding the strength through Jesus to keep you going when you don't feel like you can. That was exactly where I was—standing in the bathroom, staring at my reflection, taking that next step.

It wasn't how I felt that mattered. Feelings of weakness and discouragement would come and go, but God's Word stayed with me forever. I made up my mind: I would find joy even in the middle of pain. Joy is always there, waiting to be found in Jesus.

How do you find joy in the middle of your pain? Jesus gives us the answer in John 15:11: *"These things I have spoken to you, that My joy may remain in you, and that your joy may be full."* His joy is a gift. His joy is eternal, solid, and unchanging. That means you can wake up with joy, go to bed with joy, and carry it with you through every moment in between.

Many people confuse joy with happiness, but they are very different. Happiness is based on circumstances; joy is based on truth. The *Merriam-Webster dictionary* defines happiness as a "state of well-being and contentment" or a "pleasurable or satisfying experience." We all know what happiness feels like. It's wonderful, but it's temporary.

When I get to see my grandbabies, I am so very happy. The other day, my grandson Elisha said "*Gigi*" for the first time. I screamed so loud I probably scared him, but I couldn't help myself. I was just so excited! All my grandbabies mean the world to me, and any time I get to spend with them just makes my day. The best part is when they run up to me, wrap their little arms around me, and say *"Gigi, I love you."*

However, happiness and joy are not the same. Let me explain: if my husband comes home with chocolate—especially dark chocolate, my favorite—I am very happy (I'm really a simple girl!). However, minutes later, if I get a phone call with bad news, that happiness can disappear.

What happened? I was happy five minutes ago, but now I am sad. That's because happiness depends on circumstances, and those can change in an instant. Joy, however, is based on the unchanging truth of what Jesus has done for us. It is fixed and unchanging, which means I can choose to have joy every day. Happiness fades, but joy can stay.

Those ugly thoughts can start to creep right back into your mind if you are not careful. But the good news is this: you get to decide what stays and what goes. You have the authority, through Jesus, to take control of your thought life. There is so much power in having His joy—and the enemy knows it too.

James 4:7 reminds us, *"Therefore submit to God. Resist the devil and he will flee from you"* (NKJV). The word *"resist"* means to actively fight back. If a police officer tries to arrest someone and they resist, it means they are fighting to get away. In the same way, when we resist the devil, we are actively pushing him away. If the enemy can steal your joy, he knows you will lose your strength. And if you lose your strength, you cannot resist the devil, and if you cannot resist him, he will not flee. You have been given power through Jesus to actively resist, and when you do, the enemy has no choice but to flee.

In 2 Corinthians 5:17 it says, "*Therefore, if anyone is in Christ, he is a new creation; old things have passed away; behold, all things have become new*" (NKJV). Sometimes we stay stuck thinking about all the mistakes we've made. We stay frozen in the past and never move into the new things God has for us. God calls us to stop looking back and start looking ahead to the future He has prepared just for you.

> We cannot step into our destiny while living in our history.

It's like trying to drive while staring only in the rearview mirror. You are going to crash if you focus only on what's behind you. That doesn't make sense, right? In the same way, if we keep our eyes fixed on the past, we risk crashing into the very thing God is trying to lead us through. He has a destiny designed specifically for you, but you must lift your eyes from what was and focus on what is yet to come. Your future isn't built on your failures; it's built on His faithfulness.

"*Old things have passed away.*" That's what the Word says in 2 Corinthians 5:17 (NKJV). The problem is not that we were bad and Jesus made us good. The problem is that we are dead, and Jesus made us alive. He has beautiful plans for your life, but if the enemy can keep you stuck living in discouragement, he can steal your joy. Many of us are stuck in the past, beaten down by shame and regret. We cannot step into our destiny while living in our history. If the enemy can trap you into what was, he'll keep you from walking into what is.

Many of us are carrying around shame and guilt we were never meant to carry. It's keeping us stuck, and it's stealing our joy. We ask God to bless us, to heal us, to fill us up, but we don't give Him room to pour into us. It is like walking around with a bucket full of holes, asking God to fill it with His goodness and blessings. He wants to bless you, but He cannot pour into a vessel that keeps leaking. I believe the Lord is gently asking some of you today *"It's time to patch the holes."*

> When you choose to forgive, you make room for God...

Maybe you've been betrayed. Maybe you were hurt as a child. Maybe you are dealing with shame, regret, or a diagnosis that has left you feeling broken. These wounds are real, but if we don't allow God to heal them, they stay open and raw. It's like having a wound you keep picking at, and it never gets a chance to heal. Rehearsing the pain over and over in your mind only deepens the injury. True healing begins when we surrender our wounds fully to God.

Forgiveness does not mean pretending the hurt never happened. Forgiveness means choosing to let it go so that you can heal. It's not about excusing what someone did. It's about freeing yourself from the chains their actions tried to put on you. Forgiveness isn't for them; it's for you. When you choose to forgive, you make room for God to fill you with His healing, His strength, and His joy.

The Lord wants you to find His joy again. He wants you to bring Him the broken pieces so He can give you your life back. He wants you to hand Him that leaky bucket full of old pain so He can patch it up and fill it to overflowing (Romans 15:13). He is not asking you to fix yourself. He is asking you to trust Him enough to let Him heal you. That's the kind of God we serve!

Joy is everlasting because it is rooted in God's presence, and not in our circumstances, our bank accounts, or our own efforts. True joy comes from the Holy Spirit. When you realize that, you will understand that joy gives you strength to endure anything that comes your way (Nehemiah 8:10, NKJV). Did you know that Jesus Himself prayed for your joy? John 15:11 says: *"These things I have spoken to you, that My joy may remain in you, and that your joy may be full"* (NKJV). What an amazing promise to hold on to. Jesus wants your life to overflow with His joy.

This is what Jesus wants for you: not a life weighed down by fear and sadness, but a life overflowing with joy. However, when trials and tribulations come—and they will—it can be hard to stay focused on the joy. Notice I said hard, but not impossible. You have everything you need from the Lord to walk through this season with victory. His joy is your strength, even when your emotions try to tell you otherwise.

I said this before, but it's worth repeating: you cannot step into your destiny while living in your history. Have you caught yourself thinking, *"Based on my history, I'll fail this test,"* or *"Based on my history, I'll never get that job"*? Those kinds of thoughts slam the door shut on what God is trying to do in your life. I call it *"stinkin' thinkin,"* and nothing will steal your joy faster than believing those lies.

> ...a bad past does not mean you will have a bad future.

I was reminded of this truth during a simple dentist appointment. As I was filling out the paperwork, I came across the dreaded question: "*Do you have a history of cancer?*" I checked the box, and later, during my exam, the staff expressed extra concern because of my history. They ordered full mouth scans, not because of anything wrong today, but because of what had happened in my past. In that moment, it hit me: for the rest of my life, that little box I would check, that piece of history, would cause people to look at me differently.

The truth is simple: just because you had a bad past does not mean you will have a bad future. The enemy will whisper otherwise. He will say that based on your past history, you're disqualified from love, from success, from God's blessings, or worse yet—His forgiveness. But that is a lie! God's Word declares, "*Weeping may endure for a night, but joy comes in the morning*" (Psalm 30:5, NKJV). I am constantly reminding myself of this truth. No matter what your past says, your future is still full of hope.

There was a time, right in the middle of my cancer treatments, when I got a letter in the mail about my upcoming ordination interviews. Six months before my diagnosis, I had submitted my application to be ordained through the Assemblies of God. I had completed all the training and coursework, and this letter was the final step, which was an invitation to schedule the final interview.

I remember sitting there, holding the envelope in my shaky hands, and feeling a wave of doubt rush over me. I was in the thick of chemotherapy, sick most days, and if I am honest, I had a moment of weakness. Thoughts like, *"Am I even going to make it through this?"* and *"Should I even move forward with it?"* flooded my mind. The enemy loves to hit you when you're already down, doesn't he?

Jamie saw me reading this letter, looked at me, and said, *"You are going to make that appointment to get ordained, and you're going to keep it."* Tears filled my eyes as I nodded yes. I grabbed a pen and started filling out the paperwork, even though fear was still whispering lies in my ear. We cannot let bad moments overtake us. I knew and trusted that God had a plan for my life. Sometimes trust looks like filling out the paperwork with trembling hands.

I share this story because I need you to understand we all have weak moments. We all have days when doubt feels louder than faith. But here's the key—you can't let those bad moments define you. I knew deep down that God had a plan for my life, and no diagnosis, no fear, and no attack from the enemy could cancel it. Even something as devastating as the big "C" word would not stop the promises of God.

The day I walked into that big church to receive my ordination credential was one of the proudest—and the scariest—days of my life. I was so proud of myself for not backing down, even when everything in me wanted to. I still look at pictures from that day and see a woman who was scared but determined. I see a woman who refused to let cancer, fear, or doubt steal the future God had for her. I had a

> ...when I couldn't see clearly, I could still feel His presence...

promise from God and joy in my heart. He gave me the strength to see it through.

Did I feel strong that day? Absolutely not. Most days during that season, I didn't feel strong at all, but once again, joy isn't a feeling; *it's a truth*. My feelings lied to me often, but God's Word never did. His promises stand firm: "*I will never leave you nor forsake you*" (Hebrews 13:5 NKJV). And even on my darkest days, even when I couldn't see clearly, I could still feel His presence holding me up.

Some days, I had to look a little harder to find it. Some days were really hard. But He was always there. Those pictures from my ordination day remind me of that truth. I was wearing a wig to cover the effects of chemotherapy. I was weak and sick, yet somehow, through His strength, I stood. God didn't just see me as I was; He saw me as the overcomer He had already called me to be.

So, can you find joy in the middle of your pain? Absolutely yes. Let me also say this—you need His joy to get through it. You may be thinking right now, "*I don't know if I can do this*." Let me encourage you—you are not alone. He loves you more than you can comprehend, and with Him, you will get through it.

Remember, happiness and joy are not the same. You can find joy in the middle of pain, but you won't always find happiness there. Joy isn't dependent on your circumstances; it's anchored in the unchanging character of God. He will take what you've walked through and turn it around for your good. He has always been faithful before, and He will be faithful again.

> *Praise the Lord throughout the process.*

You just have to stay in the Word, speak life over yourself, and refuse to give in to the lies. Remember, "*If God is for us, who can be against us?*" (Romans 8:31, NKJV). You may think it is going to take forever to move past this, but God is always up to something good. One thing I've learned through every season is this: *praise the Lord throughout the process*. Sometimes His answer is yes. Sometimes His answer is no. And sometimes, His answer is not yet. But in every season—*praise the Lord anyway*.

CHAPTER 8

PRAISE GOD ON CREDIT

Most of us don't carry much cash these days—if any at all. It's just easier to use a debit or credit card when we're out shopping or grabbing lunch. One afternoon, Jamie and I went out to eat, and we used a gift card we'd been given. I wanted to bless our sweet server by leaving the remaining balance as a tip, but I didn't have a pen to write it down on the receipt. When she came back, I asked for one, but she told us that wasn't allowed anymore.

I looked over at Jamie, a little panicked because neither of us usually carries cash. He asked, "*Do you have anything in your purse?*" I said no, but I checked again anyway—and to my surprise, I found a $20 bill tucked inside my little zipper pocket in my wallet. I must've put it there and forgotten about it. Don't you just love surprises like that?

It reminded me of my parents. My momma and daddy always kept a little cash hidden in their vehicles. My daddy used to say, "*You never know when you will have an emergency and need cash.*" I'd smile and say, "*Daddy, you can just use a card.*" But he'd shake his head and reply, "*You never know, babe.*"

Well, that "you never know" moment came not too long ago. I was driving my momma's car and needed gas, but the credit card machine at the pump wasn't working. I went inside to pay and faced the same dilemma; their system appeared to be down, and they were only accepting cash—which I did not have. Then I remembered my daddy's advice. I walked back to the car, searched around, and found some bills tucked away in a hidden compartment. I was so thankful my daddy, in his wisdom, had thought ahead.

> Praising God on credit is not blind optimism; it's anchored hope.

For the most part, we all have some form of electronic payment on hand. We swipe without much thought because we know the funds are there, even if we can't see them yet. Maybe your paycheck hasn't hit the account, but you're confident it will. You trust that what's been promised is on its way. What if we approached God's promises the same way? What if we lived, and praised with that kind of confidence?

That's what it means to "*praise God on credit.*" You might not see the healing yet. You might not see the answer or the breakthrough, but you praise God anyway—not because you feel like it, but because you know He's faithful. Praising God on credit is not blind optimism; it's anchored hope. You trust that the provision is already on the way.

Praising God after the miracle is gratitude, but praising Him before it comes? That's faith, and faith-filled praise has power. The God we serve is a God who heals, sets free, and provides. But the question remains: do we truly believe He is?

Sometimes our words and thoughts get in the way, and doubt starts to creep in. Before we know it, we are struggling to believe what God has already said. But what if we do not sit back and wait on our miracle? Instead, we chase it? What if we praised God before the breakthrough? Remember, praising Him after a miracle is not praise, it is thankfulness. *True praise is bold faith in action.* It's declaring God's goodness before you see the outcome, trusting His Word even when circumstances haven't changed.

There is a powerful story in the Bible about the woman with the issue of blood. She had suffered for twelve long years. Can you imagine visiting every doctor and trying every remedy, only to grow worse with time? Back then, a woman in her condition was declared unclean. She couldn't be around people, and she was likely cut off from meaningful relationships. Her life must have felt incredibly isolated and hopeless.

She had tried everything and nothing worked. Then one day, she heard Jesus was coming to town. I imagine she was completely worn out physically and emotionally, but something inside her stirred. Jesus was her only hope. She had a decision to make: stay in the shadows or risk everything to reach Him.

People might ridicule her. Some could even call for her to be stoned. But her desperation fueled her faith. She made up her mind and said to herself, *"This is my moment."*

> ...her faith was *louder* than their *opinions*.

Most of the time in Scripture, Jesus went to the person who needed healing—but not this time. This time, she went after Him. Picture her, crawling through a dense crowd, exhausted and desperate, all while knowing everyone knew her story. She was the woman with the issue of blood. The shame, the whispers, and the rejection followed her everywhere. Yet still, she pressed through. Her desperation was stronger than her shame, and her faith was louder than their opinions.

While studying this story, one verse jumped out at me: "*For she said, to herself, if only I may touch His garment, I shall be made well*" (Matthew 9:21, NKJV). That verse always stops me in my tracks. What was happening in that moment? She didn't wait for Jesus to call her out. She didn't ask for permission or an invitation. She spoke faith into her own situation.

Scripture says she "*said to herself.*" She encouraged herself and believed her healing was coming, and she was not going to let the crowd stop her from receiving it. That is the power of declaring truth over your life, even when no one else sees it yet.

I want you to pause for a moment and think about your own life and what God is getting ready to do in it. You might be in a situation right now that feels hopeless. You may be wondering how anything good can possibly come from it. But I want to challenge you to shift your focus. Change the way you see God. Change the way you pray. Start believing that He is not only able to bring you through, but that He will. If He did it before, He will do it again. Hold on tight to that promise.

Hebrews 10:23 reminds us: *"Let us hold fast the confession of our hope without wavering, for He who promised is faithful"* (NKJV).

When we are going through difficult seasons, it is vital that we keep confessing our hope in God and His faithfulness—not just to others, but to ourselves.

> We assume our problem is too big, our past is too messy...

He is faithful to His Word, and His promises are Yes and Amen (2 Corinthians 1:20, NKJV). It is easy to believe for someone else's breakthrough—but what about your own? Too often, we assume our problem is too big, our past is too messy, or that God couldn't possibly love us like He loves others. But listen closely: *every one of those thoughts is a lie*.

Like the woman with the issue of blood, you may have tried everything. But when Jesus steps onto the scene, *everything changes*. Do not give up now—you're too close. She pressed through the crowd, whispered to herself, *"If I could only get to Jesus, I'll be made whole."* She pushed past her fear, pain, and shame. Maybe she was stepped on or shoved aside—but she kept going. Finally, she reached the feet of Jesus, stretched out her hand, and touched the hem of His garment, and immediately, the bleeding stopped. What a miracle!

Yet so often, we stop just short of our own miracle. We stop praising Him. We get discouraged. We can easily believe for someone else's miracle, but when it comes to our own lives, we start to doubt. That is exactly what the enemy wants. He wants to steal your praise before the promised miracle comes.

When the doctor first told me about the diagnosis, I was in shock. I've always believed God would work things out—but I didn't know when or how He would do it. After we scheduled the surgery, one of the doctors called and said they wanted to run more tests to determine the exact size of the tumor. They'd already done so many tests before, but now they were more concerned.

He explained that after meeting with the rest of the team, some believed the tumor might be larger than originally thought. If that was true, they would recommend starting chemotherapy first, followed by surgery. I didn't want to delay the surgery, and I definitely didn't want to hear that the tumor was bigger than they originally believed.

Many times in my life, I have said to the Lord, *"Okay God, I don't know what to do, but You do."* There are a lot of things in life we can control. You can choose what time you wake up or where to send your kids to school. But what about the things we can't control? A diagnosis? A betrayal? A loss? Those things are the things we cannot control.

When I heard from the oncologist that more tests were needed, I felt like everything was spiraling out of control. But I had to go back to the Word of God. The doctors gave me news, but God had already given me *truth*. His Word says I am healed. His Word says He has a plan for my life (Jeremiah 29:11), and I will live and not die (Psalm 118:17).

Sometimes, we need to remind ourselves: *This is just news, but it is not the truth.* Now, don't get me wrong—the doctors are only doing their job, reading the scans and sharing the results. But too often, we confuse the *news we hear* with *God's final Word.*

I trusted my doctors, and I believed God could work through them, but I had to keep reminding myself: *this diagnosis is not God's final word.* Jesus has the final say, and I have authority through Him to speak healing over my life.

> *He has a plan for my life... I will live and not die.*

So, I agreed to the additional testing, even though I felt strongly about keeping my original surgery date. Jamie and I spent days praying. We believed either the tumor would be gone, or at the very least, *smaller*. I refused to accept that it would be bigger. Then, we waited.

While we waited, Jamie said, *"Let's go out and celebrate."* I looked at him and said, *"What exactly are we celebrating?"* He smiled and said, *"We celebrating the good news we're about to*
And you know what? That sounded like a great idea to me. We trusted that God had it under control.

We got dressed up and went to a nice restaurant. When the waitress came to our table, she asked, *"Are we celebrating anything special tonight?"* I looked up at her and I said, *"Yes, we are celebrating good news that we are about to receive."* She smiled

> *I cried out... how much more do I have to take?*

politely, probably a little confused, and said, *"Oh—that's wonderful!"*

Now, why would we celebrate before we got the results? Because we trust what God says in His Word. He makes a way where there seems to be no way. We chose to praise Him before we saw the answer.

Let me be clear—this isn't some kind of "name it, claim it" faith. This is the kind of faith that says, *"Even if I don't see the outcome yet, I know God is already one step ahead of me. He has a plan. He has it all worked out. I can rest in knowing that He is my healer."* That dinner was filled with hope. We were confident that the next phone call would bring the news we had been praying for.

A few days later, the phone rang. I will never forget it—it was the same doctor who first told me I had cancer. He said:

"Well, Michelle, we have a little bit of bad news. The tumor is larger than what we originally thought. I need you to come in so we can discuss the next steps."

What?! The tumor is *bigger*! I felt like every appointment brought more discouraging news. Have you ever felt like when you're knocked down, you keep getting kicked? That's exactly how I felt. I cried out, *"God, when am I going to catch a break? I know you will get me through it, but how much more do I have to take?"*

Maybe you've felt that way too. Friend, if that's where you are today, let me encourage you: Jesus is still in control. He hasn't forgotten you. This didn't catch Him off guard. He is not sitting in Heaven saying, *"Wow, I didn't see that coming; I wonder what I should do now."* No—He owns the cattle on a thousand hills (Psalm 50:10). He sees it all and knows it all (Psalm 139:1-4).

Even when your world feels like it's falling apart, His promise still stands. You have to keep declaring that truth over your life. Don't believe the lies of the enemy or even the lies in your own mind. It is easy to get caught up in the chaos of hard seasons, but this is just a season. It will pass.

The Bible says in Psalm 23:4, *"Yea, though I walk through the valley of the shadow of death, I will fear no evil; for You are with me; Your Rod and Your staff, they comfort me* (NKJV). Notice the Scripture does not say you are *stuck in* the valley of the shadow of death. It says you are *walking through* the valley. That means you are not staying where you are. This is only a season you are in. It is only one page in your story, not the whole book.

Too often, when we're in trials, we start to believe it will always be this way. Many of us get comfortable in a place we were never meant to settle. Maybe you've accepted the lie that you'll never be healed, that your marriage will never be restored, that your children will never return to God. There comes a moment when we must stop agreeing with the lies, take those thoughts captive, and start standing on the truth.

What do you do when you have prayed and praised...and yet nothing seems to change? When the breakthrough still hasn't come? When I got the news from the doctor, I could have given up. I could have gotten angry at God and said, *"We believed. We even*

> ...don't give up hope now...

celebrated in faith, and this is what we get?" I will not lie—it was a hard season. I had to remind myself that the report was just "news." It wasn't the truth. God still has the final say.

I had a choice to make. Sometimes, I get so overwhelmed with what's happening right in front of me that I need to take a step back and breathe. I had to go back to the promises of God. I had to ask myself: *What did He say*—not *what did the doctors say*.

God asked me in the very beginning of this cancer journey, *"Are you going to trust me?"* (I talk about this in Chapter One). So now, I was faced with a sobering choice. Would I believe the enemy's lies, or would I keep praising God? Would this new information make me bitter or better? I chose to believe He was going to work all things out for my good and His glory.

God already knew that phone call was coming. It didn't take Him by surprise. So, I went back to His promises and chose to stand. It takes strength to stand on His Word—but hear me: I am stronger now because of what I went through, and you will be too. *Don't stop believing. Keep praising Him on credit, and don't give up hope now—because He is never late; He is always right on time.*

CHAPTER 9

DELAY IS NOT DENIAL

Our first ministry position was in my husband's hometown. We served as youth pastors there for five years when we began to feel the Lord calling us to plant a church about forty-five minutes away in another city. I remember feeling so nervous to talk to our pastors about it, but I will never forget how encouraging they were. They walked with us every step of the way as we navigated that huge decision.

It took a lot of faith to uproot our family from everything we had known and loved. We felt comfortable and safe at our old church. But sometimes, *"comfortable"* is not where God wants you to stay. When He began to speak, we knew we had to listen. After receiving a blessing from our lead pastors, we started taking the steps necessary to launch the new church.

Almost everything started falling into place. We found a building right away; that was a huge relief. I say *"almost everything"* fell into place

> God, this is the one...

because we still had not found a house to live in, and so we remained in our old home and drove about forty-five minutes to and from our new church every service. In this season, we had to lean in and trust in God's provision for a home closer to where He had called us.

We looked everywhere for a place to live, but the houses were either too expensive or too small for our growing family. One day, we drove around looking at neighborhoods in our church's city and drove past a beautiful yellow house with a "*For Sale*" sign out front. It was in one of the nicer neighborhoods in that city, one we had hoped to live in.

I spent so much time looking around different neighborhoods, but I kept coming back to the yellow house. I heard it was rare for a house to go on the market in that neighborhood, and when it did, it usually sold quickly. I raced home to tell Jamie all about it. He contacted a realtor to schedule a walk-through, and the very next day, we went to see it.

As we walked through the house, I fell in love immediately. It was everything I wanted and everything our family needed. "*God, this is the one*," I whispered in my heart as we walked through the house. I could already picture the kids' rooms, their furniture, and even where I would put the Christmas tree.

After we finished the tour, Jamie and I stepped outside to talk. I told him this was it; this was the house. It had the perfect layout, the perfect yard, in the perfect neighborhood. We agreed to go home, pray, and look over our budget. That evening, Jamie sat me down and said the mortgage payment would be a stretch, but with a few adjustments, we could probably make it work.

I was so excited that he was on board with what I thought was the perfect yellow house. I could hardly sleep that night, just waiting for morning so we could get the ball rolling. The next morning, Jamie called the realtor to say we were ready to move forward, but her reply stunned us. *"I'm sorry"* she said, *"it went under contract last night."*

My heart sank. It went under contract? How could that be? Just hours before we were ready to move forward, yet someone else got it. I remember thinking, "*God, do You even want us here?*" We had stepped out in faith to start this church, and now every door seemed to be closing.

It took us months to find a house we could afford, and when the "*perfect*" house finally appeared, it slipped away before we even had a chance. I was discouraged, confused, and started to question whether we had made the right decision. Was God closing doors because we had misheard Him, or was He doing something behind the scenes we couldn't yet see?

Have you ever felt like that? Like you took one step forward and got knocked two steps back? Or the more you pray, the more distant God seems? Sometimes the waiting season can be a difficult season. Maybe you're waiting on God to bring peace to a troubled mind, heal your body, or restore your marriage. You're doing the best to hold on, but it feels like everyone else is getting their breakthrough while

> Life's waiting room was never meant to defeat you.

you're still stuck in the waiting room. You may be thinking, *"When will it be my turn?"*

Waiting can be exhausting. I know we've all experienced instances when we have felt *"forgotten."* Think about sitting in the doctor's office, just waiting for the doctor to call your name. You believe you'll be seen eventually, but every minute feels like an hour. That's what waiting on God can feel like.

You trust that He's working it out, but it's taking so long. You believe it is going to happen, but you do not know when. You're holding on to hope, but it feels like forever—that's the weight of life's waiting room. You keep trusting and believing, but weariness begins to creep in.

I want to remind you, *life's waiting room was never meant to defeat you; it is meant to prepare you.* The Lord is already making a way (Isaiah 43:19). Be careful not to fall into the enemy's trap. He comes to steal, kill, and destroy the blessings God's lining up for your life (John 10:10). Your delay is not your denial. Closed doors don't always mean no; sometimes they mean not yet.

God sees everything, and He knows the perfect time for your breakthrough. His plan may not just be about you—He could be working things out for someone else too. His ways are higher. His timing is perfect. As Isaiah 55:8-9 (NKJV) says, *"For My thoughts are not your thoughts, nor are your ways, My ways,"* says the Lord. *"For as the heavens are higher than the earth, so are My ways higher than your ways, and My thoughts than your thoughts."*

When we heard my dream house had gone under contract just hours before we were ready to make an offer, I was devastated. I really felt exhausted and discouraged. However, I told myself that if God brought us to it, He would get us through it. He called us to start this church, and I had to stand on the promise that He would provide. So, we kept believing and praying. I didn't know how or when, but I believed He would provide.

Just a few weeks later, we were back in that same neighborhood, still searching. As we drove through a cul-de-sac, we saw a woman placing a "*For Sale by Owner*" sign in her yard. We stopped to talk. She was kind and open, and we really hit it off. She shared she was moving because of a divorce, and when she heard our journey of starting the church, she invited us in to see the house.

I hesitated. It looked out of our budget, and I didn't want to get my hopes up again, but she insisted, and we said yes. We walked through the house, and it was even better than the yellow house. This one had more space, bigger bedrooms, and a fenced-in yard. Jamie leaned over and whispered, "*We can't afford this house.*"

At the end of the tour, we asked the big question, "*How much are you asking for the house?*" It was significantly more than we could pay. My heart sank. We explained we could not go above a certain amount, but thanked her for her time. Jamie gave her

> **Sometimes you have to go with your heart.**

a church business card and said, "*If you are ever in the area again, come see us.*" We got in the car and left. I figured it was just another closed door. I thought, "*Okay Lord, on to the next house.*"

The very next day, she called us. I will never forget the words she said to us: "*Sometimes you have to go with your heart.*" She explained that after we left, she felt the Lord say to her to sell the house to us for the amount we could afford. We were astonished, to say the least. She asked us to come back to the house to discuss the details. When we arrived, she already had a contract prepared with the exact number we originally said we could afford.

I wondered if this was a joke, but it was not. She said "*You guys are a young family starting something beautiful together, and I want to bless you.*" That was a very thoughtful gesture. That day, we walked away with signed papers in hand. I could not believe the miracle! God closed one door in order to open the *right* door for us.

I thought the yellow house was the one. I just knew God let it get away. However, God shut that door for a reason. I learned in that experience to thank God for the closed doors in my life, not just the open ones. It is in the moments of discouragement that I must remember that God sees things we do not see. What felt like a loss just weeks earlier had become one of the greatest miracles in our journey. God sees the big picture, whereas we can only see our present situation.

While I was mourning the yellow house, God was preparing the heart of a woman who would open the right door at the right time. That is the God we serve. While you are waiting, He is working.

> While you are waiting, He is working.

Your miracle is on the way. It may not arrive when or how you expect, but it's coming because His ways are always good and His timing is always perfect. We see a powerful example of this in the story of Lazarus.

Lazarus is a man named in the New Testament of the Bible who was sick. His sisters, Mary and Martha, sent word to Jesus to come and heal him. Jesus knew this family and loved them very much. Yet, when He heard the news of His dear friend Lazarus, He did something very interesting—He waited two more days before He decided to go back to Judea (John 11:6, NKJV). Why? Because Jesus had a greater miracle in store. God's delay was not His denial. He waited on purpose.

> You cannot Panic and Praise at The same time

I know it can be hard to believe, but sometimes Jesus waits for some things to die in our lives so He can perform His miracle. God might be allowing something to end so that He can bring something greater to life, but sometimes we get in the way of what God needs to do. We need to understand that His ways are different from ours. He thinks of things we cannot possibly think about. Many times, we try to fix things ourselves, and when they

> When I think it's too late, God Gently whispers, "I still have a plan."

don't move fast enough, we panic. And here's the truth: *You cannot panic and praise at the same time.*

When Jesus finally arrives, Martha, gripped by panic, says, *"Lord, if You had been here, my brother would not have died"* (John 11:21, NKJV). That is what panic sounds like: it drowns out faith, steals your praise, and clouds your thinking.

Jesus asks where they laid Lazarus to rest. Instead of taking Him there right away, they began explaining that it was too late. Lazarus had been dead for four days, and decay had already set in.

Have you ever thought to yourself, *"It's too late?"* I know I have, many times. But here's what I've learned: God has the perfect plan. Even when I think it's too late for Him to show up, He still works it out better than I could have ever imagined. When it feels like He's forgotten us, He's actually preparing the blessing that's on its way. We just have to stay faithful and keep our eyes on Him.

When I think it's too late, God gently whispers, "*I still have a plan.*" It says in Jeremiah 32:27, *"Behold, I am the Lord, the God of all flesh: is there anything too hard for Me?"*

I believe the Lord is asking even now, *"Is anything too hard for Me?"* It may be too hard for you, but it's not too hard for God. You might be in a difficult season, but He is right on time with His plan. You may think things will never change, but when we take our hands off the situation, that's often when God steps in. We think we can "fix" problems on our own, but without God, our efforts will fall short.

When Jesus arrived at the place where Lazarus was buried, He told them to roll the stone away. John 11:41-42 says, *"They took away the stone from the place where the dead man was lying. And Jesus lifted up His eyes and said, 'Father, I thank You that You have heard Me. And I know that You always hear Me, but because of the people who are standing by I said this, that they may believe that You sent Me.'"*

> His ways are better... His timing is perfect.

Then, with a loud voice, Jesus called out, *"Lazarus, come forth!"* The dead man came out, his hands and feet wrapped with burial cloth, a cloth still around his face. And Jesus said, *"Loose him, and let him go"* (John 11:44, NKJV).

I believe He is calling you out of your grave too. You have spent years living in the past, carrying regret and shame. Maybe you've tried to be perfect for God, only to end up weary and frustrated. But He's not calling you to perfection. He's calling you to freedom. He is calling you out of your shame and guilt. He has it under control. We just need to trust Him through the process.

God could have stepped in and healed Lazarus when he was sick, but He waited so that He could raise him from the dead. The miracle wasn't just for Lazarus; it was for everyone watching too. Everyone thought Jesus had waited too long. They thought He didn't care. However, He wasn't too late. He was right on time!

The same is true for your life. God is working behind the scenes right now. You have to trust that His ways are better and His timing is perfect. It may take longer than you expected, but He is on the way. Your pain is never wasted. He will turn that pain into purpose and promotion—but you must stay the course. Even when you can't see it yet, trust that He is behind the scenes doing more than you know.

At the time of writing this chapter of my book, I am a few months shy of the 10-year cancer-free milestone. That's a big deal. I remember an oncologist once told me, *"One year cancer-free is a big deal. Five years cancer-free is a bigger deal. But ten years? That's the biggest deal."* I've held on to those words for a long time. And now, standing just a few months away, it feels like a dream.

That dream turned into a nightmare just a few weeks ago when I went in for my annual mammogram and ultrasound appointment—just like I have for the last nine years. Every year I heard, *"Mrs. Jones, you look great. See you next year."* And then Jamie and I would go celebrate with breakfast or lunch. This has happened this way every year for the last nine years. It had become a familiar rhythm; one we'd come to expect and feel thankful for. But this year, it did not go as planned.

As I lay on the table, I noticed the tech was unusually quiet, and the scan took much longer than usual. And I could feel it—something had changed. She finally said, *"Would you wait in the waiting room while I call the radiologist?"*

I said, "You found something, didn't you?"

She nodded and softly replied, "*Let's see what the doctor says.*"

> *Jesus, I pray that Gigi is brave.*

I sat alone in that waiting room praying. Thoughts raced, "*Did it come back? What did she see?*" I wanted to run out to Jamie, but he could not come back there with me. I sat and prayed. Minutes felt like hours. Finally, the tech called me back into the room and handed me the phone. It was the radiologist. I hoped to hear, "It's nothing to worry about." Instead, she said, "*I am sorry to say, but there's something suspicious. You need to have a biopsy.*"

I was numb. I could hardly speak when I got to Jamie, who was still waiting outside for me. I told him everything the radiologist had said. We sat in silence in the truck for about an hour as we waited for my next oncologist appointment, which was scheduled right after the ultrasound appointment. My doctor scheduled another biopsy, and with it, every fear and memory came rushing back. I couldn't believe I might be walking this road again.

A few days later, I got dressed for my biopsy appointment. I tried to stay calm, but fear crept in. Just before I was called back, Kristen sent me a video of my grandbabies—Sunnie, Ember, and Scarlett. The girls told me to be *brave,* and Sunnie prayed over me in the video. In her four-year-old voice, she said, "*Jesus, I pray that Gigi is brave.*" It was the sweetest reminder of God's goodness.

God has blessed me so much with all of my grandbabies, and no matter what, they reminded me that indeed God *is* with me. I wiped my tears, found my brave, and walked into that biopsy room with trust in my heart.

After the biopsy, Jamie and I did what we always do—we celebrated with lunch. We praised Him for what He was about to do. We declared, "*If He did it before, He'll do it again.*"

I *know* waiting is hard. Maybe, as you are reading this right now, you are waiting for the biopsy results—or maybe you are waiting for a job opportunity to come through. May I remind you to stay focused on the Lord? Don't let the enemy flood your heart with fear or drown out the truth.

Although I believed that God would see me through this, I am still human, and fear inevitably crept in. I had to fight hard that week. The wait was long, and the memories were heavy. But I did the same thing I've been telling you to do throughout this book: take those thoughts captive, trust God, and declare His healing.

> ...in the very middle of your pain... your praise becomes the loudest.

We were about to board a flight home from a preaching engagement when I got the notification: a new result had been posted to my online health portal. I looked at Jamie and said, "*The results are in.*" Because of the bad Wi-Fi in the hotel, it felt like forever waiting for the report to load. But, as we waited, we praised. My heart was pounding in my chest—and then the screen refreshed to display the words: "*The mass is benign.*"

Speaking the name of Jesus carries power. When words fail, His name is enough. Many times, when I don't know what to say or pray, I just speak His name. You might not see your miracle yet, but don't stop believing. Delay does not mean denial. Sometimes, it is in the very middle of your pain when your praise becomes the loudest. You may not see it now, but your breakthrough is on the way.

CHAPTER 10

YOU ARE STRONGER THAN YOU THINK

It was a year after I finished chemo that I decided I wanted to run a 5K. Now keep in mind, this is coming from someone who has never been a runner and never had the desire to be one. But something inside me wanted to prove I could do it. Facing something as frightening as a cancer diagnosis changes the way you see the world. After that, everything shifted. I started paying attention to what I was putting in my body, the makeup I used, even the cleaning products in my home. I was ready to take control of my health in a new way.

Jamie and I began training months in advance. My son Joshua, who was already running track at school, helped me along the way. He always encouraged me to keep going when we ran together. He made it look so easy, but I can tell you—at first, it felt impossible. I had to keep reminding myself: *"Do not give up. You are stronger than you think. If I could endure all those treatments and surgeries, surely, I could do this."*

> You will get through this season

Maybe that is a word for you too: You are stronger than you think. What you are carrying right now may feel like a thousand bricks, but you will get through this season. It may seem like it will never get better—but it will. God will never leave you, especially when you feel the weakest.

As it says in 2 Corinthians 12:9, *"And He said to me, 'My grace is sufficient for you, for My strength is made perfect in weakness'"* (NKJV).

As the months passed and race day drew closer, all the kids decided to run it with me. We started training together, and I realized this race wasn't just important to me, *it mattered to them, too.* It was our way of proving that the enemy didn't win. Nothing is impossible with God.

On the morning of the race, I felt strong and so blessed. Having my husband and kids running beside me meant everything. They have been my anchor through one of the hardest years of my life. I couldn't have done it without them.

When you experience trauma, it doesn't just affect you—it touches the whole family, and each person copes with it in different ways. There is no one-size-fits-all reaction, and that's okay. One thing I've learned through it all is this: don't take anything for granted. Life is precious and so fragile. We're not promised tomorrow.

So, there we were—race day, standing together at the starting line. It felt surreal. I felt strong up until the last mile of the race. That's when doubt hit me hard. *"This was a dumb idea,"* I thought, *"I don't know if I can finish."* Honestly, I could have just slowed down and walked the rest of the race. I still would have crossed the finish line. However, I did not want to just finish—I wanted to finish strong. I didn't come this far to just *"walk"* across the finish line.

> God has used every broken piece...

Jamie, Kristen, and I kept around the same pace throughout the race. Of course, my boys, James and Joshua, were already at the end waiting on us. I remember turning the final corner and seeing that big "*Finish*" banner in the distance. Just the sight of it gave me a second wind. I thought *"I can do this; I am doing this."*

As I got closer, I saw my boys cheering me on, and that's when I started to cry. We had been through so much together, and now here we were. It was just the push I needed. I can remember hugging my kids and crying tears of joy. *I did it. We did it*!

Looking back over my life, I can see how God has used every broken piece and turned it into something beautiful. On the days I've felt the weakest, He has always been my strength; and the same is true for you. God will give you the strength to face whatever is ahead. Keep your head up. Your finish line may be closer than you think. Even if you can't see it yet, it's there.

The valley you're walking through right now is not a permanent season. It's a season, and seasons change. Yes, there will be seasons of pain, silence, and heartbreak. But they are just that: seasons. Psalm 23:4 says, *"Yea, though I walk through the valley of the shadow of death, I will fear no evil; For You are with me; Your rod and Your staff, they comfort me"* (NKJV). Notice, it says you walk through the valley; you don't stay there. God never intended for you to remain in the valley.

We often think we'll never make it out, but the process is not permanent. I hear the Lord saying, *"Do not get comfortable where you are. You are just passing through this season—not settling in it."* Sometimes, you have to look at the enemy in the face and say, *"Not today, devil. You don't get to win."* But I know how it is to feel like you will never get out of the pit you are in.

I have asked God before whether I was going to make it through this trial. Two years ago, I went through the hardest time of my life, and I am not talking about the cancer diagnosis. I am talking about first losing my daddy, and then, just one year later, losing my momma. Nobody prepares you for the loss of your parents. In your heart, they feel invincible, like they'll always be there; right?

I can still remember how my sister Misti and I took turns staying with Daddy in the hospital. It was during COVID, so only one of us was allowed in at a time. Those were some of the loneliest moments of my life. I sat by his ICU bed, praying and hoping he would wake up after going into cardiac arrest.

Being in that room alone, surrounded by machines and uncertainty was overwhelming. I was feeling stressed, confused, and scared. My head ached from trying to make sense of everything the doctors were saying. I never left his hospital room; I was afraid to miss the moment he finally woke up.

One day, a doctor came in and said something I'll never forget: *"I think you need to be strong and realize your daddy may never wake up from this."* He said it so bluntly, like it was just another medical update, but to me, it shattered something inside. He delivered the worst possible news in the worst possible way. How could a doctor be so insensitive? His matter-of-fact tone felt cold, as if this was just another case on his clipboard, but this was not just another case; this was *my daddy*. There I was, alone, trying to hold it together in a sterile room full of machines and grief.

I called Jamie and told him everything the doctor said. He reminded me that what the doctor said was just news. It was not God's truth. The doctor only reported what he sees, but Jesus has the final say. Jamie reminded me to believe the report of the Lord and to find strength in that.

When I got off the phone, I began to pray. I appreciated all of my daddy's doctors and their wisdom, but they did not have the final say. Jesus has the final say. I decided to turn my fears into praise. I turned on worship music on my phone and began praying over his body. As I prayed, a peace filled the room. I still didn't understand everything that was happening, but I knew I wasn't alone. God was right there with me.

Then something unexpected happened. About fifteen minutes later, a different doctor came in. He looked straight at me and said, *"What your daddy is going through is a lot, but God is bigger."* He told me to keep praying because miracles still happen every day. His words felt like a warm blanket for my soul. They reminded me to remain hopeful.

> What your Daddy is going Through is a lot...but God is bigger

A few days later, my daddy woke up. Not only did he wake up, but he also began improving—little by little, day by day. It was a long road, but he was alive. He stayed in the hospital for more than four months before finally coming home. We were so thankful for each moment we shared.

Christmas was his favorite time of the year, and he was able to spend that with his whole family at home. How special that we had that time with him. It is something I will always cherish. Then, six weeks after returning home, he passed away.

Even though his time at home was short, God gave us a gift: precious months together, surrounded by family. Every moment mattered. I soaked it in and held it close to my heart. My momma and daddy had been married for 53 years, so when he passed, a part of her went with him. She was never quite the same.

She started to decline not long after Daddy passed. It was like her heart couldn't take the loss. She was tired of hurting without Daddy by her side. One day in the hospital, she said something to Jamie and me that made me call my sister back to the room with us. She said to me, and then to my sister, *"Girls, I am ready to see Jesus and your daddy again. I am tired."*

I knew she was so tired—tired of being sick and tired of hurting. She missed Daddy so much. It was so hard to hear those words. She had never talked to us like that before. There was such a calmness in her voice, a peace I can't describe. She wasn't afraid. She wasn't upset.

She was just ready. Then we played worship music and shared funny stories from our childhood. Misti and I would share about growing up in a home with two beautiful parents. My momma was so peaceful laying there listening to every word. A few times we saw her grin when we told specific funny stories. It was such a special time. About an hour later, my beautiful momma went to be with Jesus.

> ...what we do in the broken seasons... shapes who we become.

It was the hardest time in my life, going through two years of heartbreak, watching both of my parents slowly slip away. Yet, even in that pain, I knew God was with me the entire time.

I'm sharing this story because I want you to understand: I know what it feels like to lose someone you love. I know the ache, the heaviness, the helplessness. I know what it feels like to have the wind knocked out of you. But I also know what it feels like to find peace in the middle of pain. I was broken, but I was also blessed, and you can find that too.

I chose to look for reasons to praise Him through it all. Some days were easier than others. Let me tell you something that has carried me through more than once: when life knocks you down, God will always be there to lift you up. It's what we do in the broken seasons that shapes who we become. We all have a choice in those moments; *will we become bitter, or will we choose to grow better*?

The enemy doesn't get to control your mind, your thoughts, or your actions. You have power through Christ to choose peace even in the midst of pain. You might feel broken, worn thin, or unsure how you'll make it through, yet I want to remind you: you *will* survive this. Not only survive it, but you are going to thrive in your next season. God uses broken situations and shapes beauty out of what once felt beyond repair.

You will not stay in this valley forever. You will come out stronger. You're going to walk into a new season with more wisdom, deeper compassion, and unshakable faith. God specializes in using brokenness to bring beauty. Scripture tells us, *"The Lord is near to those who have a broken heart, and saves such as have a contrite spirit"* (Psalm 34:18, NKJV). This means if you are grieving, you are not alone.

Jesus is near. He sees every tear, every sleepless night, and every unanswered question. You are stronger than you think. Give yourself grace. Grief doesn't follow a straight path—it comes in waves. Sometimes you are fine, and then out of nowhere something—a song, a smell, or a memory—will hit you all over again, and that's okay.

I had someone come up to me one day in church and ask, *"Pastor Michelle, I lost my mom a few weeks ago. When does the pain stop?"*

I said, *"It won't completely go away. It may get easier and look different over time, but that ache will remain. What doesn't change is this: Jesus is with you through it all."*

That may not sound very encouraging in the moment, but it brings me comfort to know He's always near. Hard times remind me just how much I need Him. He doesn't promise to take all the pain away, but He does promise to walk with you through it.

Before I began cancer treatments, I remember feeling so anxious and telling the Lord one night through prayer, *"I don't know how I'm going to do this."* It all felt so overwhelming. I had four and a half months of chemo ahead of me, six weeks of radiation, and more appointments than I could count. I couldn't wrap my mind around it all. Then I felt the Lord whisper something simple, but powerful: *"Don't worry about the months ahead. Just focus on the next 60 seconds."* That felt doable. I could handle sixty seconds.

> *focus on the next 60 seconds*

That moment really shifted my perspective. Whenever I felt overwhelmed, I'd say to myself, *"I can do anything for 60 seconds, and I can make it through this."* And I would. Then I'd do it again. Maybe this strategy will help you too.

When life feels chaotic, when anxiety swells, take a breath and pray, *"God, help me focus on just the next 60 seconds. Show me I can make it through."* Then, after the minute has passed, you realize, *"If I made it through that minute, I can do the next 60 seconds too."*

I find we get overwhelmed when we start thinking too far ahead into the future. The fear of the future can bring with it feelings of anxiety, discouragement, and even depression. But God is inviting us to look up, not to look down. Hebrews 12:2 reminds us to fix our eyes on Jesus. When we focus on what we feel or what we see in the natural, fear begins to rise. Fear magnifies the enemy and puts God out of sight.

It may feel like you can't catch a break, like you're in a never-ending fight. Let me remind you: the enemy is not attacking you because you are weak. The enemy is attacking you because he knows what's inside of you. My son James once preached, *"We've given the enemy a microphone when we should have given him a muzzle."* I love that, and it is so true.

You have the power to endure whatever comes your way. Don't give up now—you are closer than you think. Without trials, how would you know He is who He says He is? Without sickness, how would you know He is the Healer? Without hard times, how do you know He is the Provider or the Restorer? Sometimes, it takes the struggle to reveal the strength of who God really is.

Be careful not to allow your past pain to define your identity in Christ. God says you are chosen, loved, and free because of what Jesus accomplished on the Cross. We are called to walk in that freedom that is rooted in His truth and not our past traumas. God has so many blessings prepared for your future.

Don't go through life carrying bitterness or clinging to old wounds. It is not worth it, and those unhealed places will eventually spill over into your relationships. When you walk around wounded, you end up bleeding on people who did not cut you. Life can be hard, but you were never meant to walk it alone. Jesus never promised ease, but He did promise to be there when the road gets rough (John 16:33).

I have said it before, but it's worth repeating: being brave isn't a feeling—it's an action. It's a decision to move forward even when the outcome is unclear. I believe you will find your brave, and you'll see that what the enemy meant for harm, God is already shaping for your good and His glory.

> *You will find your brave...*

It is time to turn the page in your story. This may be a difficult chapter, but the promise is already on its way. There is a time to weep and there is a time to laugh (Ecclesiastes 3).

In the book of Joshua, we find a powerful example of what it means to step into bravery. Moses had passed, and now Joshua was called to lead the Israelites. Joshua was afraid, yet he had to find his brave. He loved Moses and did not know if he could fill his shoes. Joshua had to shift his mindset from follower to leader. In just a few verses, God told him three times, *"Do not be afraid."* Instead, the Lord told him to be strong and courageous, and He assured Joshua *"I will be with you"* (Joshua 1:9).

This story reminds me that we can't stay paralyzed by what's happened to us. Letting go can be hard, and moving forward isn't always easy, but God is calling us to something greater. He already knows the future He's planned for you—and it doesn't involve staying trapped in defeat. You're stronger than you think and braver than you realize.

You are an overcomer, and God isn't finished with your story. If you are still breathing—He's still working. There's still purpose ahead. He has so much for you still.

> There are moments in life when we must rise up and find the brave within...

In our playroom, we have a toy with a mirror on one side. One day, my grandsons Maverick and Maddox were playing with it, and every time they saw their reflection, they would smile so big. It made me wonder: what would happen if we looked in the mirror and smiled too?

So often, all we focus on is the pain, the past, and the parts of ourselves we wish we could change. But what if we saw ourselves the way God sees us? You are strong, and you are brave. Never forget, He loves you so much.

I am believing and declaring that every person who reads this book will receive a fresh revelation. There are moments in life when we must rise up and find the brave within us. Without the struggle, we would not be the people we are today. The trials you're facing today are building the strength you'll need for tomorrow. I've said it before: today's *pain* becomes tomorrow's *strength*.

Every word God speaks has a purpose. It creates, restores, heals, and sets the captive free. You may feel right now that God doesn't have anything for you—that life is just so hard. But I want to encourage you: He has greater things ahead for you. There is a seed within you, placed there by God on purpose, for a purpose. It's often in the messy seasons of life that it feels like you're being buried.

You ask God, *"When will I see my promise? When will this pain go away?"* You may feel lost and forgotten. But I want to remind you, friend: He has a blessing with your name on it. He calls you by your name, and He says, *"You are Mine"* (Isaiah 43:1, NKJV). What a beautiful reminder that He sees each of us as His.

> God is unveiling the potential...

So, you may not see any results from the seed God planted inside you. You may feel like it's taking forever, or you may even doubt that God cares. However, a seed that is planted and a seed that is buried *look* the same on the surface. Both are covered in dirt—hidden and unseen. But one is buried to be forgotten, while the other is planted to grow.

What I'm trying to tell you today is that you may feel buried under the dirt. You may feel buried under the weight of the world. However, that pressure you feel is producing potential in your life. What you see as a place of death, God sees as a place of purpose. There is purpose in your pain. You will overcome, and you will make it through. He has something beautiful waiting on the other side of your pain.

God is unveiling the potential and promise in your life. It never happens in the timeframe you think it should, but His ways are always perfect. His words aren't just ink on paper; they are His promises. His words are powerful and true. They are sealed with His faithfulness, sealed with His love, sealed with His promise, and sealed with His blood.

You thought it was over and that it could never get any better. Some of you have experienced broken promises and disappointments in your life. People have walked out on you. People have stabbed you in the back, and you've lost loved ones, leaving you feeling empty. What I'm trying to say is this: hold on to His word—even if your life looks buried, even if your situation feels hopeless, even if you get a bad report from the doctor. When everything in your life feels like it's over, God says it's not over. He has a promise for you, and your story is just beginning.

> God doesn't just bless what is coming... He redeems what was lost.

No matter what you are facing today, His promise still stands. When you face hard things, He will not let them overtake you. I know it can feel overwhelming, and you can feel tired, but you are closer than you think. Don't give up now. When you feel like your world is falling apart, hold on to His word. Your breakthrough may be closer than you realize, and God is faithful to finish what He started in you.

It is not over. It is just a season, and it will pass. You will come out of this fire, and you will not even be burned. You may be in the valley season right now, but God sees what was taken in your life.

The enemy thought he had you, but greater is He who is in you than he who is in the world. God doesn't just bless what is coming, but He redeems what was lost. Your blessings are coming.

If you are reading this right now, remember you are not alone. The enemy wants you to feel like you are all alone, but that is a lie. You are more than a conqueror. You will make it through.

As of July 2025, I will be 10 years cancer-free. I made it—and I'll continue to make it—not because of anything I've done, *but because of who lives in me*. If I can get through it, so can you. So, stand up, dust yourself off, and find your brave. Your brave is strong. Your brave is beautiful. Never give up. Keep going— I am cheering you on.

VERSES AND REFERENCES

People often ask me which specific scriptures I prayed during the hardest seasons of my life. Below are the verses I placed all around my house and spoke out loud every single day. My prayer is that, as you've read through this book, you have felt encouraged and strengthened in the Lord. I pray that courage has risen within you to unveil your brave and believe, deep down, that you can overcome this trial. No matter what you face, you are never alone.

Scripture Verses

Psalm 138:3
In the day when I cried out, You answered me,
And made me bold *with* strength in my soul.

Psalm 56:3
Whenever I am afraid, I will trust in You.

Psalm 34:1
I will bless the Lord at all times;
His praise shall continually be in my mouth.

Isaiah 41:10
Fear not, for I *am* with you; Be not dismayed, for I *am* your God. I will strengthen you, Yes, I will help you, I will uphold you with My righteous right hand.

Psalm 118:17
I shall not die, but live, and declare the works of the Lord.

Hebrews 13:8
Jesus Christ is the same yesterday, today, and forever.

Psalm 91:16
With long life I will satisfy him, and show him My salvation.
Mark 9:23
Jesus said to him, "If you can believe, all things are possible to him who believes."
3 John 2
Beloved, I pray that you may prosper in all things and be in health, just as your soul prospers.
Psalm 107:2
Let the redeemed of the Lord say so,
whom He has redeemed from the hand of the enemy
Romans 8:11
But if the Spirit of Him who raised Jesus from the dead dwells in you, He who raised Christ from the dead will also give life to your mortal bodies through His Spirit who dwells in you.
Isaiah 40:31
But those who wait on the Lord
Shall renew their strength;
They shall mount up with wings like eagles,
They shall run and not be weary,
They shall walk and not faint.
Jeremiah 29:11
For I know the thoughts that I think toward you, says the Lord, thoughts of peace and not of evil, to give you a future and a hope.
Matthew 11:28
Come to Me, all you who labor and are heavy laden, and I will give you rest.

Romans 8:25
But if we hope for what we do not see, we eagerly wait for it with perseverance.

Joshua 1:9
Have I not commanded you? Be strong and of good courage; do not be afraid, nor be dismayed, for the Lord your God is with you wherever you go."

References

Leaf, Caroline. *Who Switched Off My Brain? Controlling Toxic Thoughts and Emotions.* Nashville, TN: Thomas Nelson, 2009

www.ingramcontent.com/pod-product-compliance
Lightning Source LLC
Chambersburg PA
CBHW061748070526
44585CB00025B/2834